UNBOUND

UNBOUND

COMPOSING HOME

NAYT RUNDQUIST
EDITOR

New Rivers Press is a nonprofit literary press associated with
Minnesota State University Moorhead.

Cover design by Angela Konz
Interior design by Nayt Rundquist
The publication of *Unbound: Composing Home* is made possible by
the generous support of Minnesota State University Moorhead,
the Dawson Family Endowment, and other contributors to New
Rivers Press.

NRP Staff: Nayt Rundquist, Managing Editor; Kevin Carollo, Edi-
tor; Travis Dolence, Director; Trista Conzemius, Art Director
Unbound book team: Brenna Brastad, Ivon Diaz-Perez, Amber
Finneseth, Shaina Garman, Angela Konz, Cheyenne Musolf
Office Interns: Brenna Brastad, Amber Finneseth, Shaina Garman

 Printed in the USA on acid-free, archival-grade paper.

Unbound: Composing Home is distributed nationally by Small Press
Distribution.

 New Rivers Press
c/o MSUM
1104 7th Ave S
Moorhead, MN 56563
www.newriverspress.com

Contents

Tillandsia, Totoro & "Mono no aware"

Roughly 650 different plant species can be categorized as *tillandsia*. Air plants that do not root in soil, they've got spindly bits that help them cling to their surroundings. Most commonly found on tree branches & power lines, *tillandsia* have leaves covered in trichome cells that allow them to absorb water & nutrients from the air around them. Since competition for soil-based resources is so fierce, *tillandsia* are mobile, floating as seeds on their dandelion-puff parachutes 'til they find somewhere to cling with their spindly roots. Moving around a lot as a child meant they couldn't lay down roots the way other plants do—only grasp on for a year or two & absorb their needs through their trichomes until *tillandsia*'s father was re-stationed. Forced to untangle their roots from the tree or power line or fence & parachute to the next destination to re-cling for a time, try to figure out how to digest the moisture & nutrient sources in their new climate.

***

I often find that I get homesick for things I've never actually experienced. Summers as kids with a ragtag gaggle of misfits, racing around your hometown on bikes—pointless, grand, defining adventures. Knowing friends for decades—having been present for every stage of their development—knowing their families as your own. Having pride—ownership—belonging of a place. Having roots, deep, burrowed down over generations living in one town—one area. Roots that communicate, share nutrients, caring, information across mycelial networks. Knowing the names of people as they pass on the streets. What is it like to have such a deep understanding of such a tiny section of the planet? A specialization of a location? I've known swaths & patches. Found my nooks & crannies. Carved out & clung to little areas to call my own for snatches of time. But that deep-in-your-gut longing for a house—a hometown—a place where roots commingle toward mantle—I don't have that. But I do feel all I've missed out on. A longing for those connections—those familiarities—that belonging.

***

Moving so often meant I saw a lot of the world, but I never really had a solid, lasting connection to a physical place. I haven't truly recognized any buildings or towns as *home*. There's no place I can look back to & say, That's it. That's where all my memories are stored. That's where I grew up & where all my friends are from. I never really landed in a place solidly for a long stretch of time. So, I can have base camps, maybe. Houses or apartments rented & shallowly rooted in for a year or two, but nothing that felt permanent.

I once had a theater friend tell me he wears a character as lightly as he would a hat, & that's largely how I see home as a physical phenomenon. For most of my life, *home* was a location I could wear as loosely as a hat & discard without care. A hotel, a tent, a friend's apartment have all been *home*. Often, the word simply means 'wherever we slept last—a temporary locale to rest, relax, eat, & store our stuff for a bit.' When traveling, 'Let's go home,' just means 'I'm tired. Let's not be here anymore—let's be back at that place where I can sleep.'

So, people are more home to me than places. Folks I've gotten to know very well & feel comfortable with. Whom I can relax around in the same way—I imagine—many people feel going back to their childhood homes, stepping back into the bedrooms where they grew up. Where they learned of themselves & how to be human.

***

For a year or so, when almost all of us lived in the same area—paternal grandparents, aunts & uncles, cousins, parents—we had Home Church. Rotating monthly-ish gatherings to discuss topics tied to faith & spirituality across denominations & religions. A place to talk & laugh & eat—to keep close in a hectic modern world & be together.

My grandfather had also been in the army, so Dad & his brothers had been *tillandsia* too. This family had clung to each other & thrived. Grown apart—lived on opposite ends of the country—across oceans—for years. Then drew back together, homing to each other, trichomes attuned in similar directions. They're as much home to each other as any place could be.

In much a similar way, my wife has become home to me. We've weathered hard, dark times—curated & cultivated our energies, our collective environment. Though I rarely have much connection to physical spaces, the emotional & energetic landscapes we build provide a haven from the wild forces of the world. She is home.

***

In his short story "Mono no aware," author Ken Liu writes about the sensation of the awareness of the fleeting beauty of the universe—of everything being finite—that everything will end. He describes the sensation as like a kitten licking your heart. When I first listened to LeVar Burton read the story on his podcast, I cried. I *wept*. There was finally a term to put to how I feel about home. The only way I understand a familiarity—a belonging—but a sense that I can't hold on forever.

The ache I get when I cycle through YouTube videos for music I listened to ten, fifteen years ago. Familiar waves of emotion & longing—of teenage angst & directionlessness. Of wandering barefoot through rainy backroads with just a discman in tow. Of wondering where life would take me next.

The melancholic comfort of watching *My Neighbor Totoro* on repeat for months after my wife's & my second miscarriage—reassurance that even this suffering, this grief will abate. That some day will eventually be more than crying in the car, crying on the couch, clinging to each other crying. That even the soul-deep, body-wracking suffering of loss will recede, as impossible as it seems in the moment.

The kitten-heart-lick feel of recalling homes past. The shelter & base-camp they provided us, transitive though each may have been, served their purposes. Led us further in their own ways. The stability & ability to curate an environment allowed us to grow as artists, as humans, as a family.

***

Folks have asked me why I have such a fond connection to stories—to books & comics & movies & shows. One part is that I love visiting new worlds—seeing places I've never been—places that can never be—exotic & exciting locales. But I've lived that—I've moved to new places on a near-yearly basis. I've visited deep dark forests & sprawling metropolises—wandered cities where I didn't speak the language—picking up snatches as I went. It's really the people I love visiting. Rogue & Kurt—Frankenstein's Monster—Frodo & Sam—Lilith & Akin—Prince Ashitaka—Binti & Okwu—Ishmael can come with me wherever I land. They're the same no matter where I end up—immutable friends—a tree branch in every locale my spindly roots can cling to. The stories of grand adventures & lovely people were my consistency—my safe place to land. I've watched & read & lived in those stories—with those people—countless times.

***

I've always been a sucker for found family stories—tales of misfits banding together to be for each other what none could be for themselves. I've spent my life assembling, discovering, excavating found families—building enclaves in which I can feel at home, since I never had a solid, consistent physical location to root in for long. No real place to belong. My longest-standing found family is one I've cobbled together from the characters in my books—in the stories I carry along in my heart. As my obsession with narratives bloomed & I shifted into my role as managing editor at New Rivers, I realize that I built another family here—a new home in the narratives & works of my writing friends & family—in their words, in their minds, in their lives. That's what these pages amount to: an assemblage, a gallery, a collage of a few members of my writerly found family. A tribute to how they grapple with their own understanding of *home*—juxtapositions palimpsestic, vibrant, & polyvalent. Beautiful & resonant in the ways they are themselves. Reading their homes has helped me understand my knowing of the word too.

Hopefully you, dear reader—I've always wanted to write that—can find a home here too, or find some new understanding within these pages.

—Nayt Rundquist
Spring 2022

UNBOUND

Erin Slaughter is the author of *A Manual for How to Love Us*, a short fiction collection forthcoming from Harper Perennial in 2023, and two books of poetry: *The Sorrow Festival* (CLASH Books, 2022) and *I Will Tell This Story to the Sun Until You Remember That You Are the Sun* (New Rivers Press, 2019). She is editor/co-founder of *The Hunger*, and her writing has appeared in *Black Warrior Review*, *CRAFT*, *The Rumpus*, *Prairie Schooner*, and elsewhere. Originally from Texas, she is a PhD candidate at Florida State University. You can find her online at erin-slaughter.com

In the Heart of the Heart of the Heart of

A town is a kind of grief. Not the pain of childhood, but the imprint of that helplessness. How it can sneak up again if you ever let yourself stop moving.

Anna, the small North Texas town where I grew up, a blip on the map an hour south of the Choctaw Nation, was built on the commerce of truckers passing through, their spots at the torn vinyl booths of Driver's Diner filled hours later with others the same as them; everyone going and seemingly never going anywhere.

The sepia-tinted road that leads, möbius, past truck stops, vacated ditches, subdivisions made of the same gray brick, the same cherry-stained plywood; the town's one stoplight near the train tracks and the convenience store costing teeth on teeth for a pack of Twizzlers, the nearest market another thirty miles; a rain-rusted, drive-in malt shop owned by the family of a friend of a friend whose neighbor hung his wife in one of the crumbling houses out back; the equipment trailer repurposed as a catfish restaurant repurposed—I swear—as City Hall; the single ancient elementary, middle, and high school of the city limits, jeweled with portable trailers where the football coach fumbles math equations; field pocked with the impact of boys' bones, where semi-yearly the circus stumbles through, elephants kicking up dried maggots from the barren soil and bringing police out to observe the decades-long burn ban; town named for the pale daughter of a rail-conductor, like the next town over, and the next town over.

I left my homeland quickly, my footprints marking the front yard with ashes on the way out, but Anna still lurks in my blood, breathing heavy as cornstalks. A story I can never outrun, its shining eyes follow me across the sinew of highways.

Being gone was never a choice for me. It was a lust for disappearing, a flame tangled into my DNA. My bedroom window had a view of the highway, a thin string stretched above a valley of gray shingles replicated across angled roofs. I'd sit awake and count the cars whose headlights flashed across the sky, the roar of engines like faint lullabies in the distance. As soon as one appeared, it was gone, and the bright call of another replaced it. My thoughts followed them to wherever they came from, wherever they would go. I longed to join the spectral fleet of anonymous travelers who left without realizing that where they had been was Somewhere. That someone briefly saw their fractals of light and wished to know them, wished to be them.

Looking back, I've spent my life dreaming desperately of escape, without knowing why, or to where, or from what. These are the things I do know: I worked at a call center one summer in college, and the only thing I remember about those two months of dial-tones and sanitized headsets is the map above the gray cubicle where I sat. The year I was twenty, I fantasized extensively about faking my own death, Sherlock Holmes style. Even when I walk down the street with a friend, it is always a few strides ahead, as if my body is itching to break away.

I know now what it's like to follow isolated, winding roads through forsaken-looking small towns with names like Post and Tucumcari, a chorus of hollow historic buildings left in their wake, echoes of a time when the road sang out and the towns vibrated with life. I want to tell you how it felt, driving through the desert at ninety miles an hour, flat endless nothing to all sides; head blazing with the ghost of Jack Kerouac, utterly free and accountable to no one except the yellow divider leading onward, the pink sand from the mesas that sweeps over the asphalt. The sense that if there is a God, it most certainly resides in West Texas, in the winking light of the orange sun flickering through the trees as it saunters out of view like a celestial headlight, in the iron orchards of abandoned cars and rusted drive-in signs.

***

When I travel, it is rare that I do not travel alone, and if I am with someone else, even someone I love, it is rare that I don't wish I were alone at some point during the journey. It's certainly more convenient to have a traveling companion: there is the strict comfort of company, and someone to take pictures of you doing silly, touristy things at opportune moments. Waiters don't look at you strangely when you have another person at the table to share dinner with. But when you're experiencing the world alongside someone, you bounce your perceptions off of one another, and the person you're with becomes as much part of the place as the place itself. Traveling alone, observing this planet fresh and foreign, is one of the only ways we might connect with who we are, what we think, and how we move through the world when we are contextless.

But no one truly moves through the world without context, or without a daisy-chain of ghosts trailing behind them. First, the context through which you have the option to travel depends on, among other factors, the body you are born into, and the cultural system that defines how you are freed or limited to move through the world inside of it. When I visited my family between trips or moves, my mother would tell friends and neighbors where I'd gone or was planning to go, and the women in the room would inevitably reply with some cocktail of fear, pity, and amazement, "Oh, wow, I could *never* do that alone."

I'd tell them that yeah, they could, if they had a bit of money and a car and childcare, they could take a weekend trip for themselves. There were websites where you could find places nearby, things to see along the way, plan it all out. I recognize the privileges of childcare and money to spend are not accessible to everyone, but for these women, they were. Still, they insisted: they couldn't go alone, they wouldn't know how, they wouldn't enjoy the silence, it wasn't safe, they just hadn't ever done that sort of thing, *women* just didn't do that sort of thing.

Reflecting on these conversations, I'm reminded of a passage from Sylvia Plath's diary:

"My consuming desire to mingle with road crews, sailors and soldiers, barroom regulars—to be a part of a scene, anonymous, listening, recording—all this is spoiled by the fact that I am a girl, a female always supposedly in danger of assault and battery."

Though I was not able to escape so many of the burdens and scrutinies imposed during girlhood, somehow, I didn't internalize its limits of mobility. Or perhaps I was so motivated to leave Anna and live some kind of elsewhere-life that I blindly burned past them.

Yes, there was the drunk man who harassed me in a coffee shop and followed me outside to the parking lot on a transient night in Pocatello, Idaho; and there was the tow truck driver who found me gasless in the middle of the night, twenty miles outside of Roswell, New Mexico, who could have easily knifed me out of existence in his truck cab; yes, girls and women disappeared, in body or in mind, after what was done to them on the road. But when I began traveling alone,

I was either too young to understand what there was to protect myself from, or to understand myself as something worth protecting. In a sense, I was looking to disappear, anyway—to lose myself in order to become myself, to escape the body and life I was told must be mine, but could not be fully mine.

In Ancient Greece, *hysterical* was the word for how the uterus was believed to wander around the body, aimless. All women's rage, sorrow, fear, mania, was said to be caused by this wandering. If only she'd stay put. If only there were a way to chain her to her body.

***

I have seen snow piled on cows' backs like lumps of sugar. I have seen sulfur smoke rise up from pastures under a ghostly lavender sky. I have seen the ground beneath me cracking like unloved taxidermy. I have seen gutted neon motels, and a snakebird perched on the nose of an alligator underneath a crumbling bayou bridge. I have seen phosphorescents skitter across the Puget Sound, and slept in a driftwood fort by the water's edge. I have touched castle walls in Ireland and felt the echo of pasts reaching back. I have traced shorelines from memory, from the front bow of a ferry, as if in a childhood dream. I have seen delirious sunsets over four different coastlines and understood them to be eternal, have watched the landscape bleed from desert to mountain to bright green, mossy grave. I have reached through a broken window in Memphis and pulled out a lipstick-kissed card with a disconnected number for the Greyhound. I have foraged for a skeleton key by the Barren River in Kentucky and thrown it into Wisconsin's Fox River three years later, fireworks blurring the sky to gunpowder. Summer rain filling the Hudson Valley as I paced half-naked in the hallways of a haunted wooden mansion. The bleached bone of the Mojave at 110 miles an hour, January cracking my windshield. We move through the world as the imprint of everyone and everywhere that has entered us. We put down grief for the last time, only years later to pull it from between our teeth.

***

At twenty-five, staring out from a rooftop pool at a sherbet-orange sunset spreading across Tampa Bay, I realize every mile behind me, every box of clothes I've hoisted across the country, every city I ran from or burned through or tried to love until it broke me, has been an attempt to honor and destroy the ten-year-old child I was—following the headlights across the sky, dreaming of a someday when I was anywhere, anyone, else. The lie and the beautiful ecstasy of the gone that whispers: *Orphan yourself.*

I'm trying to say, I think, that the women I know write with fire under their skin because there is a fire under their skin. Maybe their words were ignited by some man—father or lover—who made them feel the lightness of grief, or tried to drown them in remembering. Or maybe women are born of fire and spend their lives clawing their way back from burning, creating new stories and lives to tend the shame of singeing everything they touch. How telling it is that we describe creation as a kind of obliteration. Here, I am writing myself out of the record, and perhaps I have always been. This is just another kind of leaving.

**

The first time I stayed with my parents again after moving away, I stood in the bedroom I grew up in, my former fortress, where the air was full to the brim with memories of sleepovers, tears, laughter, friends, fears, first loves—now vacant. The lime green walls bare, scarred with a decade of staple marks. The exciting and unsettling aura of a life condensed neatly into cardboard boxes. It was the realization that home is not a place, but a feeling, the ember of a flame inside you that must be nurtured. The house still survives, but home no longer exists, except in faded memories.

Perhaps that's what I've been struggling to escape to, if anything: home. I've searched for it in bleached hotel sheets, in foreign countries and foreign bodies, in the pounding of wheels on pavement. I've caught a flicker of it from time to time: in a sandwich shop in the bone-cold rain, a galaxy of milk being poured into hot tea, the line in that glorious song when Paul Simon sings, *"Losing love is like a window in your heart..."*

Escape, like home, has rarely been about running toward something, and more often about running from it. I would like to believe it's a craving for new experiences alone that keeps me constantly moving, unsatisfied with limitations of place and time. For some, that's enough to keep a bag packed in the trunk, a flight schedule open. For me, it isn't about escaping from a place; it's escape from my small, choked voice, the responsibility of *being*, from my very skin.

Life moves, eroding everything in its path, until a child is grown and sitting in an airport, wondering what made her want to leave so badly in the first place. Knowing she will not return unchanged.

***

In the spring of my first year living in Florida, I was invited to give a reading at a bookstore in Dallas, an hour south of my hometown. It had been five years since I'd last crossed the state line into Texas. Since I'd left, both of my college roommates got married and had babies, and my remaining friends moved away, or moved in with one another and adopted grumpy, beloved chihuahuas, or moved into Dallas high-rises that gave them a glimmer of gone, with the comfort of being able to slip easily back into the past.

I drove fourteen hours through the night from Tallahassee, and early the morning of the reading, merged onto I-75 toward Anna. That day happened to be the vernal equinox, the radio informed me between over-produced country songs: the one day of the year when an equal amount of sunlight spreads over every place on Earth. A day, perhaps, when all places shine more brightly, even the ones that formed us.

The thin gray road in my memory was now beige and widened to five lanes, and filtered by my lack of sleep and the strange morning light, driving it felt absolutely alien. I never thought I'd live to see the day when Anna gained a Walmart, but there it was, right off the truck-stop exit, next to the lot where they tore down Driver's Diner to build a Whataburger. A sandstone wall now stretched across the back of my old neighborhood, blocking the backyards and their flimsy brown fences. But as I drove toward what was once the town's single stoplight, deepbright spots of memory called out to me, pockets of space that shone as if from déjà vu, hidden among the ugly growth of strip malls and concrete fences: the Texas Star Bank, whose lobby we rented out after business hours for my youngest sister's baby shower and my thirteenth birthday party. The Coyote Den convenience store where my friends and I stopped along the drive to school to buy expired bottles of Snapple. The brick building with "Beech Nut Bacon" painted in yellow on the side, empty as ever beside a new baseball field. Even the cornfield I lost myself within at twelve, my first attempt at escape that left me grounded a whole summer, was razed of its vast mystery, the field shorn.

I stopped to buy a butterscotch shake at The Malt Shop, the rusted ice cream sign one brilliantly unchanged thing. Standing in the gravel lot felt like past lives—like retracing, as if I'd only just remembered it existed, the *realest* life, sunk deep at the bottom of me, barnacled and fading, now excavated clear and true. Like a heartbeat, my mind reverberated: *This is my homeland, I am of this place.* I wanted to reach down where I stood and fill my mouth with a fistful of the dry dirt.

That night, at the reading in Dallas, my high school best friend, Dylan, showed up with Phoebe, his partner of ten years—who he spoke to for the first time via MySpace messenger, sitting at the computer desk in my parents' room after school while I lounged on the sagging bed beside him. We tramped through Deep Ellum streets and bar patios and taco stands, the moon like a wildflower bulb grieving brightly in the sky. When Dylan and I recalled how my mom kissed him on the beard when she was drunk, how his dad held garage sales at our house as an excuse to flirt with my mom, how we skipped school and sat on the back of my truck smoking soggy cigarettes in the rain when his Nana died, I realized: you can tell your stories to anyone, but there are so few people who know the shape and smell of them, whose precious broken years are intertwined with your own.

We reached the gate of Dylan and Phoebe's downtown apartment, and my heartstrings snagged on the dwindling minutes. I think I felt then what I've heard other people describe feeling with their families—normal people, whose family relationships aren't bloated with layers of shame and guilt. To be among people who've known the many iterations it took you to arrive at this spot, who see those pasts in the face of the person you are now. People with whom, after however many dislocated years, that love and that knowing resumes effortlessly.

Earlier that day, as I left Anna, I turned into the side entrance of my old neighborhood. I parked across the street, in the driveway of the now-vacant house where my stepdad lived before meeting my mother. The door to our old house was painted bright blue, a ceramic frog in the entryway, my mother's birdbath plucked from the yard. I wondered how it would feel to go inside, to see those small pockets of *mine* swallowed in the overwhelming *not-mine*, like I'd seen all over town. I knew by the next time I returned, those few glimmers of the dreadful, magical town I was raised in would be snuffed out, and so I knew that I would not return.

As I stepped out of the car, my flip-flop broke. I bent over to fix my shoe when a car pulled into the driveway and a dark-haired woman got out, walked up the path, turned the knob of the sky-blue door, and disappeared inside. I got back in my car and drove away.

***

I want to tell you about ascending the narrow stone steps, so steep it required clinging to a frayed rope as I shoved my body toward the sliver of sky above. At the top of the thirteenth-century castle is "The Stone of Eloquence," and like many things Irish, its origin is winding and legend-filled: it was bestowed to Cormac MacCarthy by a witch he saved from drowning, or was used as an "oracular throne" to decide royal rulers, or was the deathbed pillow of a saint. For as long as The Stone has been in residence at Blarney Castle, the story has been this: press your lips to it, and receive the gift of otherworldly speech.

When it was my turn, I lay on my back on a rubber tarp. A slight Irish man wearing a windbreaker and a patchy goatee struggled to fit his arms around my thick torso. He told me to grip the metal rails on either side of my head; all there is to do is lean backwards, and slot your upper half into a hole that could tumble you head-first onto the green, green, faraway ground.

I couldn't do it. My fear of heights took over, and I couldn't trust that gap of blank space not to suck me under. I wished for the courage, tried for a number of minutes to force it while the man encouraged me: *Reach back, lift your head, kiss, you won't fall.* But just as when I climbed to the top of the high dive at thirteen, and the space between myself and the blanket of chlorinated blue expelled me like the wrong side of a magnet, I was frozen in place. The man, getting exasperated as a line began to form behind me, suggested: *Maybe just reach back with your hand, if you can do that. Just touch it. That's good enough.*

I wanted to make this into a myth about my hand imbued with that superstitious magic, to let you believe that pressing my fingers to the stone, instead, brought the gift of eloquence to my writing. But you should know: it was only because I was too afraid to lean over the edge, to trust the arms that held me, to stretch my mouth out to history and receive its mystic kiss, that I had to build this story. That I had to learn how to claim a different kind of voice.

Darius Atefat-Peckham's work has appeared in *Poem-a-Day*, *Indiana Review*, *Barrow Street*, *Michigan Quarterly Review*, *Zone 3*, *The Florida Review*, *Brevity*, and elsewhere. He is the author of the chapbook *How Many Love Poems* (Seven Kitchens Press). His work has recently appeared in the anthology *My Shadow is My Skin: Voices from the Iranian Diaspora* (University of Texas Press). Atefat-Peckham grew up in Huntington, West Virginia, and currently studies English and Near Eastern Languages and Civilizations at Harvard College.

Lesson

Bibi shoves another nameless voice   to
my ear. They live there beneath the lobes. *Talk,*
she says. My fingers cover hers as I take the
receiver. This, the staple of our visits: my Bibi
holding the telephone to my ear, feeding me
basic *tārof,* one heaping pile after another on
my plate. Tārof is *extreme* politeness,   a
lovely way of lying. This, the fluency I pray for.
For the first time in my life, I can understand
their native tongue on my own. I can respond
somewhat in kind. *You look so much like your
mother.* They say. *I am so proud of you.* They cut
in and out. *Ghorboonet bream. I die, I destroy myself. For you.* I talk   to my Papa's last surviving sister on Whatsapp Video, wondering how
she made it all these years, upside-down and
muted. When I run out of words to say, I run
across carpets to wear my great-grandfather's

hat. Bibi calls it *kolā-namadi*. I say it. After a few tries.   My hair curls up beneath the basin like vines, the hat fits snugly on my head. I nod my head in mock-prayer. *Oh Dada, that's bad!* I feel how I did as a boy. My great-grandfather and I had the same sized head, I think. I laugh. They die for me. I tell myself I've only been studying Persian a short-while. Farsi, I correct myself. Ammeh says I speak beautifully. This is *tārof.* I tell my Ammeh. That I am trying, still.   *inshā'Allah, inshā'Allah, inshā'Allah.* The hat stays snug. I say I am glad to have spoken to her, instead of *with* her. How to say *these* are enough for the day. Never enough. *Someday I'll go to Tajikistan*, I say. Someday maybe Iran. It sounds like a threat. I tell my grandparents I need to be immersed. As in, a shipwreck.   I sound angrier than I mean to. My grandparents are silent. They are unimpressed, thinking of home. Never enough. *Anyways you are doing amazingly good,* Bibi says, still wrestling it from her tongue. I want to take their home and have it for myself. They die, they destroy themselves. For me. This dying, a life-long practice. I don't have to live if I don't want it. I don't have to grieve at all.

Half Something I Am, Half Something I'm Not

Bibi offers me a Persian carpet. She teaches me to choose the only one she doesn't wish to part with. *Everything is for you.* I am entitled to everything. To be half-silk. To prove her right and wrong again and again as, on the plane-ride home, my knuckles turn white around the handles of my bag. She teaches me to be suspicious of everyone. Remembering how, after shopping for me, Bibi would count up the price-tag of all I was wearing. She'd joke that I couldn't walk through New York or Tehran like this, Darius the Great in gold around my neck. One day, she jokes, she'd buy me a Rolls-Royce, so I could roll up to my mansion, my home, like the king I am. There is a home like this near me, owned by the only Iranian

I've ever known in West Virginia. I know there must be others. He loves me, buys me a book about the American coup against Mossaddegh. I tell him that somehow, my grandparents love Mossaddegh and the shah and America, all at once. He nods his head gravely. I am missing something, of course. *Khali, khali,* he keeps saying. Looking out into this man's sprawling yard, I feel joy and uncertainty. I am so privileged, so lucky, I've forgotten how much. I am ashamed. I didn't used to care about money. I tell him I want to speak perfect Farsi, that I want to work for the government. I will always be a poet, a writer, I tell myself quietly. It didn't used to be a secret. He writes me a beautiful inscription on the inside of my book. He speaks perfect English, so perfect his family teases him for it. He hasn't been in Iran since he was thirteen. He used to live in the garden in the back of a church. For a moment, as he hands me the book, I see the beginnings of things and their endings, the ghosts of flowers turning their heads. I look into his yard. I see a Persian Garden, though it isn't there yet.

Tara Ballard is from Alaska and is currently pursuing her PhD at the University of Nebraska–Lincoln. She is the author of *House of the Night Watch*, winner of the 2016 Many Voices Project and published by New Rivers Press. Her work has been published in *diode*, *Michigan Quarterly Review*, *North American Review*, *Salamander*, and elsewhere. In 2019, she received a Nazim Hikmet Poetry Prize.

Home-Coming: A Zuihitsu

And then the Turkish coffee.

Days like this I want to graft myself to a table in a corner of the restaurant on Lake Otis and Northern Lights and order all the demitasses— that the tabletop may be covered in five, eleven, twenty-one dark liquid mirrors.

Outside on the balcony: it is 9:00 p.m., sun high in the sky. Seventy degrees Fahrenheit with light pouring onto our shorts and tank tops, which, admittedly, I could not have worn so visibly prior.

I read somewhere that culture is simply how humans make a place meaningful—how our species cultivates significance like gardeners.

A bumblebee dances around strawberries hanging from a basket. She buzzes an audible hum. In their pots, our chives and chocolate mint.

We will sit outside until midnight. Maybe I will grab a long-sleeved shirt, maybe when the heat slips behind the neighboring rooftops.

When I read the definition of a *zuihitsu*, I cannot help but think of Charles Simic and "The Necessity of Poetry." How he does not clarify the need for the genre, not once. This tells me that there are times when it is appropriate to not refer to one's purpose.

In a different text, one I borrowed from a shelf in the Anchorage Museum's library, Richard Lewis writes, ". . . when life . . . [in the North] is reduced to its barest essentials, poetry turns out to be among those essentials."

In a territory my country deems "conflict," I once had a sixth grader shout, "Everything is poetry!" and fling his hands to the sky. The truck driving down an empty street late at night with one headlight. The raven fighting with the sparrow above cottonwood. Dandelions that grow despite pesticides. The child who rubs rosemary. Cloud movement. Cloud presence. A pot of lentil soup. Quiet after an air raid siren. A welcome sign.

The Anchorage Museum exhibit: *Everyone Is Welcome Here*. A sign reads: "Between 1980 and 2017, Anchorage's . . . immigrant population grew by 180.4 percent." Another: "Immigrants and refugees contribute enormously to the culture and economy of the state."

My husband and I too were immigrants— though Americans tend to favor themselves "expatriates" (thus indicative of how words and connotations create [dis]comfort)—as we left ours and spent eight years elsewhere.

Another exhibit, running alongside the *Welcome*, revolves around food culture and the impact of immigrants on the local food scene. In this hall, entire bookshelves of cookbooks greet guests. Recipes are framed and hang on walls. There is a couch that looks much loved.

One of the cookbooks is titled *The Immigrant Cookbook: Recipes that Make America Great*, compiled by Leyla Moushabeck. There is more than one reason to love this title, something to remind us: each background as vital as ingredients in my father's goulash.

When I brush the cover of Moushabeck's cookbook, I think of movement. Human migration; individual, paired, mass. The sound of feet lifting off runways, the sound of trains across open spaces, boats that make it to shore. The stamp at passport control.

What does an empty home, an empty apartment look like? A bite of the lip as the once-resident closes the door behind them.

I guess, in some way, I am (now) new here. This present, continuous season—that of home-coming and adjustment—is a time when I experience many firsts: the first snow, the first dipnetting, the first harvest of salmonberries, the first walk through fallen leaves.

I have been back for one year now, exactly. This means, according to some theories, I have seven more years before I feel wholly back again. Seven, in some cultures, is faith, is the number of completion.

Spruce trees "have four-sided needles that roll easily between the fingertips." Sprinkle a handful of fresh tips in a teapot; add water and boil. Steep for five minutes. Strain and serve as a beverage high in vitamins. Dry needle tea can be used to purify the blood.

As a child, I remember reading a study that hypothesized, even in the year 3000, the population of Alaska will not surpass one million individuals. To my elementary school mind, this was a relief. To my adult mind, it is even more so.

The name *zuihitsu* is derived from two Japanese kanji: "at will" and "pen."

We had no address. We were the metal door with the garden after the L in the road just beyond the corner store. We were the gate in the walled compound where paved road becomes red dirt and a family of goats trundles come evening. We were the door across from the school where girls came to receive an education.

We returned to Alaska. I wanted to make mint tea. I went to the store, looked in the produce aisle, and found parsley, cilantro, plastic packages of basil. I asked one employee where the bundles of mint could be found. There was no such bundle. Three stores and the same result. Now we grow our own.

In *Forces of Imagination*, Barbara Guest writes, "This landscape appears solitary and yet there in the short grass is the hidden person placed there by the writer who desired a human instrument to bear witness . . ."

I often feel myself needing to be quiet.

A few days ago, my husband and I made the drive to Hope. While he fished, I sat in a chair—tall grass behind me, the creek before me, mountains everywhere. We were alone with the sound of water, plink of his hook as it broke the surface.

I asked Google how many inspirational quotes there are about wandering. Various results had different numbers. Goodreads says there are 168. A few travel sites narrow it down to 75. Pinterest seems confident there are but 44.

I am sure there are different lessons to be learned from a) wandering and b) returning to the terminal from whence we came. Some lessons, of course, are immediate. Some lessons, it seems, do not reveal themselves until we have driven years down the road. I am still learning.

Mutabbal requires two medium eggplants; two (or six or ten) cloves garlic, chopped; tahini; a few tablespoons of lemon juice; the always-pinch of salt; two spoons olive oil; fresh parsley, finely chopped. Prepare a charcoal fire or the eye of a gas stove. Stand eggplants upright, stems attached. Balance, turning frequently, until soft. The skin should darken, crinkle. Rinse with cold water. Peel off the skin. Remove stems, chop flesh, and drain in a sieve. Combine eggplant and garlic to a mash.

Add tahini, lemon juice, and olive oil. Blend until creamy. Then parsley. Pulse. Taste. Serve with flatbread.

Our dear friend lives in Hawai'i. Has been in the U.S. since 1948. Told us, when moving, you will experience the four *H*s: honeymoon, hostility, humor, and home. Regardless of the move across town, across territories, across oceans. He forewarned: the four *H*s are not doled out in equal increments, like quarters in a basketball game. It is easy to slip back into an *H* you presumed already having moved beyond.

A slight breeze comes. The branches of spruce trees near our balcony lift and rustle.

It is said that King Herod enjoyed swimming pools, creating bodies of water in the middle of desert. Close to the Judean Wilderness, a visitor will find the Herodium, a man-made mountain fortress. At its base, there are the ruins of a pool, complete with what was an island in its center. When one walks across what would have been the pool floor, one will find a plethora of small squares the size of Scrabble pieces. These are the many fractured points of a mosaic, spread fully across the once pool. If one bends down, touching, a pale smudge will be left on the thumb.

And what in our lives is not a mosaic? What in our lives is not an innumerable amount of limestone pieces fit carefully together to create a complete art that, from a distance, represents a clear shape, an identifiable form?

If Canada geese fly overhead, I will not examine their V, will not guess what direction it is they are headed, choose not to make a prediction.

When visiting the museum archives, it is important to exercise immense care. Wear blue rubber gloves when handling negatives and lowering dark strips of film to light. Choose a seat along the windowsills and, while you dig for something you are unsure of finding, keep in mind that is life on the inverse of glass. There are flowers. There are piano keys and sunshine and a child laying in the grass like a starfish.

What could we do with all the words for *home*? I wonder if we collect them all. Paint the side of a building downtown with as many as we can. Stand back and speak each word aloud. Notice which words chime within us, register comfort in the way we pronounce them, in the movement of lips. Home, dwelling, abode. Habitat, domicile, residence. Return.

My head against my chair, eyes shut. Light turns my lids red, and I shiver in the late warmth. My husband settles in his chair beside me.

From Eva Saulitis, a gentle offer: "Maybe I'll sing. *Last night I had / the strangest dream*. Of the woods / I thought I knew so well."

The longer I am here—I am living—the more I tangle. There are many things I do not know.

But what I do know well is this:

Jehanne Dubrow is the author of nine poetry collections, including most recently *Wild Kingdom* (Louisiana State University Press, 2021), and two books of creative nonfiction, *throughsmoke: an essay in notes* (New Rivers Press, 2019) and *Taste: A Book of Small Bites* (Columbia University Press, 2022). Her writing has appeared in *Poetry*, *New England Review*, *Colorado Review*, and *The Southern Review*. She is a Professor of Creative Writing at the University of North Texas.

This Phone Call Is Being Recorded

The mustard-colored telephone on a high table in our living room often rang like a small air raid siren going off. Sometimes it was my grandmother calling from the States, once to say the doctor had found a dark uncertainty in her breast. Sometimes it was a colleague with news about the steelworkers striking up north. Sometimes it was what my parents described as "a contact."

When I was alone, I liked to lift the phone from its cradle, imagine I was speaking with someone at the Embassy. This meant nodding my head and listening to the dial tone with great concern. I made a serious face like my father's, my mouth pinched into paleness. "Hmm," I said. If I stood this way long enough, a taped message on the other end of the line would interrupt my pretending. "This phone call is being recorded," a voice said in Polish. "This phone call is being recorded."

For me, the news was always secondhand—something my parents told me using words a child might understand. "The government is angry," they said. Or they said, "People are fighting to be free." *Solidarność*, I knew, was Polish for "Solidarity," which meant standing united together. "Like this," my mother said, interlacing her right hand with her left.

For me, the news was that afternoon I saw people on the streets lifting their arms into the air, making a V with their fingers. My parents said, "It means victory."

Once, when I was seven, we drove across the Vistula River to watch a movie in the basement of the Embassy. The film was projected against a long white wall; "E.T. phone home," murmured the small alien, lifting his bright finger in the air. I understood telephones, how the long spiraling cord can connect us to voices faraway.

I did my best to remember everything I heard. *I could be a recorder too*, I thought. If I just listened closely enough, I could make permanent what my parents called the news, their worried talk in another room, the shuffled whispering of papers on a desk.

The Blanket

The afghan on my bed—a bed "for a big girl," my parents say—has red and white squares, thick knotted loops of yarn that feel soft against my face. I like to lie beneath the blanket and splay my hands. I stick my fingers up into the pattern so that the afghan shifts and moves as though it has come alive, like it's reaching for the ceiling.

When there are thunderstorms, I pull the crocheted throw over my head. Then I can watch the lightning through the openings in the design. The blanket contains thousands of these tiny windows.

When the weather is quiet, I turn my head to the side and place one of my ears against the afghan. Now the openings are cracks I can listen through. I hear my parents in a room down the hall. Sometimes the television talks for hours. Sometimes the house makes conversation with itself, argument of wood and glass.

The only time I hate the afghan is on nights when I listen to the music of the boy and the wolf. I don't mind the flute that chirps like a bird or the oboe quacking like a duck. The cat is a clarinet and very sneaky with his padded feet across the meadow. But the wolf is a terrible sound of brass, "French horns," my father tells me. When the cassette stops playing, my parents kiss me goodnight. My mother pulls the blanket to the edge of my chin. The door closes.

Then I can feel the holes in the blanket. They are big enough to let a hungry wolf crawl through.

The Voltage of That Moment

The electrical outlets in Zagreb were dark holes, the right size and the correct height from the floor to fit a baby's finger. I had just learned to crawl, pushing myself backward, a contrary motion that allowed me to see what I was leaving but never where I was going. Reaching the opposite end of the room, I would stop when the soles of my feet brushed up against the wall, my arms and legs tired from long travel. I might sit then, rounded and slightly leaning, at the edge of the carpet.

My father tells me, that when he saw me stretching toward the outlet—that mysterious circle full of current I couldn't understand—his hand moved to slap mine in a blur of instinct and fear.

"No!"

One moment, I was still. And in the next, my father says, my face crumpled. I slumped forward, my head touching the ground as if I were bent in prayer. I began to sob.

It was the first time someone I loved hurt me. Although he knew the slap had saved my life, and although I would never try touching one of the electrical outlets again, my father says he never forgot the voltage of that moment, how close I had come to danger and what it felt like to watch me *crumple* in my new knowledge, that the world betrays, even in trying to rescue us. It is a place that both injures and electrifies.

Photograph of My Mother

I am guessing from the thinness of her face, that I must have been almost three when this picture was taken. I have to guess, because I lie outside the frame. Perhaps I was asleep, curled tight against my blankie, its silken edge kissed softly to my hands. Or else I stood at the French doors that looked out onto the backyard, a place I was not permitted to wander—there were mambas coiled in the grasses, vipers the color of spring leaves. She would have been thin from breastfeeding me well past the usual age that, in those days, pediatricians permitted. I had almost died of some tropical disease; I fell ill during the rainy season when the tin roof of our house was the sound of thousands of fists knocking. A small baby, the sickness made me smaller. "Keep her on the breast," the doctor said, "and bananas, as many as she will eat." For decades after, I couldn't smell the yellow fruit without choking on what I remembered of its taste, banana mashed with the back of a spoon, banana crushed to softness on a plate. As for the breast milk, I can't recall it, although the doctor said it saved my life. The photograph shows only my mother's face, which even here is beautiful, the amber light a tenderness against her skin. She is smiling. She is smiling as if the body is not a pane of glass, as if the body is a sheet of metal and nothing can get in.

Travis Dolence is a librarian at Minnesota State University Moorhead and the former director of New Rivers Press. His work has appeared in *Water-Stone*, *Rock and Sling*, *The MacGuffin*, and *Burningwood*, among other publications. In addition to an MFA, Travis holds master's degrees in Library Science and Geography.

Interim Dead

Digging my own grave I find bones, animals mostly.
Anatomies, sown into soil, foxed brown, bleached white.
Color palettes of ultraviolet exposure, mineral leaching, water intrusion.

Here lies the king pelican spine, fine and ivory as any instrument,
now silenced from the marsh and cane, the interim dead, half-way
decomposed, disassembling, embarrassingly caught in partial transition—

from thing to nothing, a featherless architecture holding only its own weight.
In the voids of eggshell-skull, I see myself as a fellow flightless traveler,
fortunate enough to walk this side of the grass along the riverbank.

Re: Grandmother, The Huntsman, et al.

Here's the trick to getting through the woods:
remember that everyone you love is the Wolf,
each devouring part of you—
not out of malice, but necessity.
    The need to consume,
        The savagery of loss,
            The annihilation of memory.

Also, remember that you, too, are the Wolf
    haunting another's dark forest,
        hiding behind every copse of trees,
            taking what you need without regard or intent.

This time you are Red,
    and I am the Wolf.
Next time you are the Wolf,
    and I am Red.

Together we will arrive
at the forest's edge—
still hungry, still full.

Duende (Let's forget depression for solace)

Let's find ourselves as bees,
    flirt with flowered wallpaper,
        fight fireflies in hanging fixtures.

Let's look back on violence and see beauty,
    visit graveyards of youth,
        find comfort in duty.

Let's wave off reunions,
    bury sentimentality under the tallest tree,
        abandon our loneliness on a high shelf.

Let's forget depression for solace.

Let's graduate from walking to flying,
    escape the wasps of this world,
        open new avenues in our hearts.

Let's discuss love instead of losses,
    discover new benchmarks,
        persist until complete.

Let's turn circles together.
Let's fall to the ground.

Weatherhouse

Paint the tired clapboards Finland.
Paint the cracked porch Mining Town Sky.
Wear the watery clothes of Superior,
the dust of dirt roads.
Let's move west, travel over topography lines
fine as your red hair, close as fingerprints,
real as the cartographer's pen—
Elevations rise as bread loaves, as breasts.
Put both arms around everyone.
Listen to the autumnal wind in high branches—
deciduous needles of tamaracks rain down
on our truck's hood like golden splinters, as if the sun
were throwing sparks to the forest floor.
Let's not mound up words into inky piles,
hide from each other in their shadows.
Reflections of the weatherhouse
played back to us, a slow photon scatter.
In the end, let winter find us edge-tumbled,
worn soft by experience.

Joel Peckham is a poet and essayist whose nonfiction has appeared in many journals, including *Brevity, River Teeth, The Sun, and Under the Sun*. He is the author of seven books of poetry and two collections of nonfiction, including *Bone Music* (SFAU) and *Body Memory* (New Rivers). With Robert Vivian, he is co-editor of *Wild Gods: The Ecstatic in Contemporary Poetry and Prose* (New Rivers). In late 2022 his spoken word collection, *Still Running: Words and Music*, will appear from EAT Poems.

The Ghosts of Summer

There is something inherently uncanny about a summer camp—especially one that has been around for more than half a century. Every boys and girls camp in America is a ghost town for ten months of the year—snow piling on the roofs of empty cabins in the winter, grass growing knee-high over ball fields in the spring. Maybe a lone groundskeeper-and-caretaker roams the property, dog by his side, chasing animals from the offices, bats from empty lofts—alerting the owners if a roof caves in or a pipe bursts. I remember visiting Camp Manitou once in the winter with my family while we were on Christmas break. This was early on in a ten-year hiatus between my only summer there with my first wife, Susan, and my hobbling return as a widower in 2004. Darius must have been only one or two years old. But what I remember most was Cyrus in a bright red snowsuit sitting in a sled with his cousins Drew and Natalie, all of them laughing as I pulled them along the road, through the woods, down to the flagpole area. As a boy I had always thought it would be wonderful to sled down that hill with the cabins forming a corridor on either side and the lake below. But it wasn't. It was alarmingly cold and empty. Too steep. Too fast. Too scary. And without the campers and the staff, without the bugle calls, everything shrouded in white and gray, the place just felt wrong. Off. A breaking of the illusion of permanence, of the world that only existed when we hopped off the bus to laughter and hugs in June and piled back on in August, sunburned and sad.

Too much like the camps across the lake that failed in the early '80s. The ones we'd sometimes visit in the ski boats in the waning last few days of summer (what we called "the dying times"), when there was little on the schedule other than packing and cleaning and the unit leaders had to be inventive in finding ways to entertain the kids and keep them out of the cabins and off the courts as they piled up with trunks and duffle bags. I remember walking around the grounds of Camp Lakeridge fifteen years after it had closed its gates forever. Everything about the place was eerie. I remember the cabins that had caved in from too many seasons unattended. I remember the rust-red flakes of paint floating on stalks of uncut grass. Piles of docks stacked beside the waterfront, waiting for a summer that never came. I was twelve years old and felt as if I'd just walked across my own grave. All things pass, for certain. But they also repeat, time looping back over itself.

Summer camps are a place of ghost stories told at night, flashlights pressed beneath the acned and peach-fuzzed chin of the storyteller. Every former camper and counselor knows a variation on a chilling tale of wild-men and hermits creeping out of the woods to steal children or cut off an errant arm hanging below a mattress, of boys being pulled down into the darkness of a murky lake during swim period. It doesn't matter that few camps could survive the actual death of a camper—the world being the litigious place it is—every camp has a story "the directors don't want you to know about." About the curse of Old Bunk 7, its ruins rotting in the woods behind Bunk 6, the ghosts of its campers still trapped within, or Bunk 13 sunk into the ground during a rainstorm, boys trapped eternally in the mud, or the haunted piano in the theater that plays in early hours of the morning all on its own, its keys pressed by the ghostly fingers of a theater director's daughter who, fifty years ago, had fallen one summer from a catwalk to the concrete floor twenty feet below. All of it is nonsense of course. Old Bunk 7 does sit back there, pushed among the pines to rot after a winter storm caved its roof, but its only occupants are raccoons. There never was a Bunk 13 (why tempt fate?). And the theater building, though ominous when empty at night, was built in the early '90s and all of Manitou's theater directors have been bachelors and bachelorettes, most of them gay and childless. They did catch a hermit—a man who lived off the grid, in the woods, in tents and lean-tos, stealing what he needed from local backyards and sheds. That news set off a storm among ex-campers on Facebook. But he never hurt anyone. And as far as we can tell, he never came to Manitou—at least not in the summer.

To return to a place for two months of every year is to constantly be reminded of the past while facing absences and change, ones that accumulate too fast to manage, and remind us of how blindingly fast our lives move. It's like watching people dance beneath a strobe light at a club. Everything leaping across the gaps—too fast for the brain to process. Constantly catching up and trying to make sense of the darkness and how these images connect to each other. Life as a flip-book.

It's been twenty years since that brief visit and three years after my last summer directing the music program at Manitou and the place still haunts me. And writing this I feel almost as if I'm standing there at the top of the hill as the winter cold burns my cheeks, the old fishing lodge looming at the bottom of the hill, the office across the way, thinking of how I'd run through it as a little boy, chased by Ellie, an overwhelmed and apologizing babysitter, my swim trunks in one hand, my sister Tina pulled along in the other.

I still remember exactly where they kept the best candy for the "canteen" and the best toys from the lost and found, both sharing a long dark corridor walled with cubby holes on either side, masking tape labels announcing, "Charleston Chew", "Twizzler", "M&M", "Flashlights", "Batteries", and there were baskets of fishing rods and nerf footballs, contraband squirt guns and jackknives (confiscated from deep in some child's duffle bag). At the beginning of every summer, my mother and I would rifle through clothes that no one had ever claimed the previous season—not only camp apparel but sports equipment, books, and electronics. We'd check for tags and if the camper was no longer on the list of returning boys, she'd black the name out with a sharpie and write mine in its place. It never bothered me that so much of what I owned was secondhand. That I was wearing some rich kid's clothes. It never occurred to me, really, because in a cabin where everyone had to follow the same rules, those class distinctions were easy to ignore. As I combed through lost treasure I could hear my father's booming voice, gravelly even then, upbraiding some counselor who was "dumb as wood" or "didn't know his ass from his elbow" in the back room where he sat at a large circular table that made me think of King Arthur. It was either a privilege or a terror to be called "to the back of the office" over the P.A., depending on what my father, the athletic director, wanted to speak to you about. I was not allowed in that room most of the time, so I'd avoid it, sometimes poking my head into the office of Uncle Bobby Marcus, a long-limbed young man still, though prematurely balding with a terrible comb-over. He had just purchased the camp from his older brother, who had inherited it from their father, and he seemed caught between the shock and joy of the responsibility. Always on the verge of laughing or screaming, eyes bulging like Marty Feldman's. "Jo Jo, what are you up to now, you little knucklehead, *yooou* idiot." I loved him. Back when Uncle Bobby was just a photography counselor, he used to lope down to our little suite of rooms in the large moldy fishing lodge by the lake, a guitar slung across his back so he could sing "Drunken Sailor", "Zoom Gully Gully", or "Puff the Magic Dragon" to us before we went to bed. My sisters, Lisa and Tina, would beg him to "please stop" and would crawl all over him as he fumbled with the chords and laughed. My sisters tell me he had a terrible voice but I don't remember it that way. I just remember thinking that "Puff the Magic Dragon" was the greatest, sweetest, saddest, song I'd ever heard. And whenever I hear it, to this day, I go back to that little bed in that little room we shared, the three of us, together.

My father was the athletic director all those years and for most of them, my mother ran the ski program. So, from 1970 to 2018 my family seemed a permanent part of Manitou. And our name is still stamped on it— literally—affixed to a to-scale replica of Fenway (Citgo sign and all) dominating the playing fields, PECKHAM PARK painted in three-foot-tall white block letters across its own Green Monster.

And that sense of belonging, of continuity, was much of the reason why I returned after the accident that took Susie and Cyrus from me somewhere on a desert highway while on Fulbright scholarship to Jordan. Darius was only three years old, and I was asleep in the back seat when our touring van drove into the sand-truck parked across Kings Highway somewhere between Amman and Aqaba. I was knocked unconscious. I did not see my oldest son thrown through the windshield. I did not witness the emergency crew arrive to pull me from the wreck. I did not ride with my mother-in-law in the helicopter with Susie. Or watch as the light passed from her eyes. I did not hear the sound of Darius crying—his leg broken, his brother and mother gone, his grandmother rising above and away from him as he was trundled into an ambulance. I did not hear the helicopter blades buffet the air around us all. I woke in King Hussein Medical Center, suddenly a single parent and widower, crippled, lost in grief and trying to pick up the fragments of his life. And with the future uncertain, lonely and frightening. It seemed like the most natural thing in the world to go backward. Back to a place where Darius would have 400 brothers and I could lean on my father. A man as solid as a stone and built like one, limping behind him until I could walk again.

It took a few years to make my own place for myself there, but my apparent ability to play three open chords on guitar while singing qualified me to create and build a music program. So with a budget of about $250, I bought some used electric guitars and a bass, salvaged an old Yamaha keyboard, reassembled a drum kit from pieces I found underneath a stage and went about establishing my own little *School of Rock* among the pine trees of Oakland, Maine.

I remember the first time I tried to run a practice with my new music staff, Davis McGraw and John Salvage on lead and bass respectively, and Tristan Hewett—a talented Australian we borrowed from the waterfront—playing the wobbly old kit we'd salvaged from the theater building. We tore through

"Have Love Will Travel" by The Sonics, and the sound we produced in that echo chamber, bass-heavy and driven full blast through our pawn-shop amps and equipment, was like a jet taking off. At that point in my life, I had only played music with other people one or two times, and it was fun, but this was something else—hard charging, alive, distorted, and loud as hell. I knew I was a lousy guitarist, but I could sing a little, and so could Davis and John. And if my acoustic-electric, running through the P.A. was lost in the mix, all the better. I could feel the music vibrating all along my body as I flailed at the strings and screamed away. My nerve pain disappeared, and the darkness pushed back—and for a few minutes I was a kid again singing along with my friends in my father's cavalier with the volume turned all the way up—a version of myself that wasn't about grief or loss, not because they didn't exist or because I was ignoring or avoiding them. But because they stopped being the center of my consciousness, that hard black stone was particalized and charged with electricity, lit in the glorious noise we were making and out of which we are made. I loved being lost in the mix.

For a long time after the accident, returning to Manitou every summer to play rock star was stabilizing—a way to connect the threads of life. I married Rachael and we spent the summers there together, throwing parties for my musicians at our place some nights and others, sipping wine with my mother and father as he yelled at the Red Sox. The program grew and grew, the equipment getting better, the music getting better as Darius became a camper then a counselor, working both on my father's staff and then mine. Rachael and I made something of a home there. And for a while, it worked.

Until it didn't. The threads began to snap. And did so, so gradually I almost missed it happening. Another director from my father's generation used to say, "It's a tough place to grow old." And it's true. The camp may be pushing seventy-five, but the campers and counselors are perpetually young. Very few people have jobs that allow them to take the summers off, which is why the staff is made up mostly of directors who are in education—like me and my father—and counselors who are incapable of holding down regular jobs, are in that brief liminal moment between college and entering the workforce, or who live non-traditional lifestyles—wanderers who equate rootlessness with freedom. So many restless souls come to this place to land for a couple of months and play Peter Pan before leaping off again to the next adventure—not always reaching the other side of the chasm. I became an expert at falling in love and saying goodbye. At best, that meant getting very close to someone over eight weeks and then wishing them well, wondering if I'd ever see them again outside of their Facebook photos. But there were darker endings: the beloved waterfront director who died of brain cancer, the special events director who shot himself in his car, parked in the driveway of his daughter's house; old family friends who disappeared into alcoholism, drug abuse, and mental breakdowns. And then there was

Chase—the staff member and former student who I was certain would write twenty books, acknowledging me, his teacher, in every one, and who could play anything on his guitar. Whose voice sounded almost exactly like my own when he sang and could fit into mine in perfect harmony. He even had the same blue eyes and blond hair, and I felt, for a moment, like he was sent as recompense for the child I lost—only to die, asphyxiating on the floor of his apartment above his father's garage—a hypodermic needle six inches from his hand.

But the hardest loss was and still is the long good-bye I was saying to my father. For the first sixty-five years of his life Joel Peckham Sr. was the smartest, sharpest, best-looking, most talented, most respected, most feared, most important person in the room, no matter what room he was in. But by the summer of 2018, he couldn't remember the names of his players on his varsity baseball team. And when he started threatening to punch other directors in the mouth, forgetting the innings, the outs, the time a game was supposed to start, when each moment he stared blankly at me through wide, ice-blue eyes, silently asking me to tell him what was going on, I knew that something was ending, that you can keep returning to a place but not a time. And it was long past time.

Sometimes we write past the ending, so enamored with our story that we can't tell if it's over. I had always been a bit of an outsider at Manitou, uncomfortable with the frat-boy culture, experiencing the place one step removed, refusing to be part of anything that didn't involve a guitar or a baseball bat. But every day of that summer, I felt like a ghost in a graveyard. I wasn't sleeping well and was going to bed later and later. Drinking too much bourbon, smoking too much weed, waiting to lie down until I was so wiped out I couldn't avoid sleep. Until I was certain it would slam into me like a train. Then I'd be out, fitfully dreaming for five to six hours before the sun poured into the cabin, my eyes fluttering open until I rolled out of bed to start it all over again. I felt old and lonely. After thirteen years of coming to camp with me and our Golden Retrievers, Rachael and Darius finally decided enough was enough. Rachael missed her house, her bed, and her freedom away from bugle calls, communal meals, the dust and noise of food trucks arriving at 6 a.m., or buses rolling in at 11 p.m., and the flood of testosterone everywhere. And Darius wanted to have one summer with his high school friends before starting college. "I fully support you going," Rach told me. "But I'm done."

So I went it alone. Running my program *and* my father's. Setting up the day's practice in the band room then running the twenty-five yards to the baseball diamond to help my father. Then back again. It only made things worse that both the ball field and the band room reminded me of Darius. And everything in that cabin reminded me of Rachael—from the paper lantern hanging from the rafters to the vintage blue-velvet fold-out couch we purchased at a consignment shop, to the tall blue bookcases, to the sail-like sheet draped along the ceiling. All speaking to her eye for design. Her nearly absurd attempt to give this place a sense of home. But without her there, without Darius, it couldn't be home, even for the summer.

Most of my life has been in tension between holding on and letting go. Catch and release. I have lost a child and a spouse. And I have remarried. I lost jobs and left them. And friends. And lovers too. I have moved from state to state. Home to home. Sometimes I think I keep moving so the past can't catch up with me. But there's just no way to travel far enough or fast enough. And I write essays and poems, books of them, about it all. Compulsively turning over the same material. Trying to get it right. Thinking I've done so. And then I write them again, changing the titles, rearranging the words. And the mind has a way of stitching it all together without bothering to make any sense of it. I still have dreams in which I am ripping into the Beatles *Please Please Me*, Chase Adkins singing and playing lead but suddenly becoming Reid Moak or Andy Ambat. And the drummers keep changing too, Tristan to Reuben to David to Miles to Julia and I am desperately trying to switch tempos and keys, forgetting the words, the chords and harmonies. Or I'm swimming at night in East Pond with my sisters and my boys, and we are all young, shuddering with cold and laughter. Dripping with moonlight.

I spent so many years at that place, trying to make something, build something—nothing with *my* name on it—but something that could grow and live beyond me, long after even I'd forgotten it. And it had forgotten me. The way one song contains so many other half-remembered melodies.

Maybe this is what it means to be haunted. Not the same thing coming back to you again and again. Not exactly. It comes back, but is always changing, always in disguise. It is *almost*. Almost the thing you remember. Recognizable but strange. Uncanny. And you can't stop staring at it, searching for that part of yourself it offers up. Dreams of Heaven and nightmares of Hell may be a psychological response to our fear of death. But ghosts are a different matter—they speak to our fear of being forgotten. Of disappearing from the worlds that we create. Of being erased. And our inability to imagine them going on without us.

Julie Gard's prose poetry collection *Home Studies* (New Rivers Press) was a finalist for the Minnesota Book Award, and additional publications include *Scrap: On Louise Nevelson* (Ravenna Press) and two chapbooks. Her essays, poems, and stories have appeared in *Gertrude*, *Clackamas Literary Review*, *Blackbox Manifold*, and other journals and anthologies. She lives in Duluth, Minnesota, and teaches writing at the University of Wisconsin-Superior. www.juliegard.com

House in Parts

Wall

I love a full house, most of all when I am alone in the other room. I love the sound of people I love gathered and laughing, playing a game, eating together, the clink of dishes being washed and dried and put away. I love having guests I know well enough to go off and take a nap.

As a kid, I would often go up to my room. The house was always full of people, which is maybe why it feels strange now that it's not. It's been a lifelong adjustment to a smaller family. I think of so many of us scattered out this way, into more compact units than the ones we came from, living alone or in pairs, or in threes with a child who grows up and moves away. Not so often now the feel of occupied rooms and me alone in mine.

I can conjure it though, a house full and walls solid and stretching. All the inputs are manageable, and the sounds coming through from the other side are soothing and familiar. Even a voice raised in tension is diffused—disturbs the peace a bit, but from here there's no need to address it. I can read a book in solitude but know that my loved ones are near. I feel closest to them, and to myself, when we're alone together.

Screen

My brother and I had bedroom windows on perpendicular walls, stone with the windows set deep in them. Past bedtime I heard him talking to his small green G.I. Joe men, lined neatly on the sill. They were rarely at battle but more often planning. It was summer so our windows were open, the air gridded by fine metal screens in the house we had just moved into. He wasn't a face but a voice behind layers of dark. We talked quietly and the children ran the house, at least in this corner. His voice was so gentle, and I hear him now in his son, that precision and care. We whispered through the screens, over the crickets. We said each other's names.

Nail

I pound one into the hard plaster wall of my daughter's new apartment. Her solid 1960s building is in a mostly older, quainter neighborhood. The outer walls are cement and I'm glad for the sturdiness, the protection. She has made a home of it, put many of her pictures up, but not yet the bright diptych of trees her friend painted. These need to go on the plaster expanse of the inner wall, and she takes out small gold nails and a compact, sturdy hammer. We hold the canvases up together, her other mom telling us when to lift or drop. I make marks with a pencil. I ask her if she wants to hammer and she doesn't, so I do.

In the lamplight, I hold the little nail with its sharp end against the wall and hit its peg end. Firm as a woodpecker, *tap tap tap*, but I am off the mark and the nail slips. I get my thumb good and chip the plaster in a long white scar. I climb down to search for the nail on the television stand and find it hidden in scattered silk leaves, for our daughter is a decorator. There is color everywhere, in strewn blankets and vases of seasonal flowers. She has made her own home now, does almost everything on her own. I am glad to do one small task, that my daughter will let me.

Hinge

Old door, squeaky hinge. As I open the front bedroom door, the squeak dips down and then up like the tonal flow of a question in English, a long, drawn-out phrase where the asker knows the answer they want to hear. The opening door is a question with an agenda. The closing door is an answer with no agenda. The hinge's creak as it closes is worldly and resigned, like our dog's sigh as he settles on the couch.

This hinge has been painted and repainted. Flecks of orange show under cream. Each end is a small, light orb. A pin holds the hinge together at its joint. The plates of the hinge are almost invisible behind all the paint, the tops of screws with their flat divots mere suggestions. Could these flat, inlaid hinges be one hundred years old like our house? They are still useful under their layers.

The other side of the door frame, I notice, the part that swings in air, has been gnawed by the cat to bare wood, punctured by her small, sharp teeth. This is her room most of the day because we have to keep the animals separate. Our pets are apart yet connected by a cord of energy between their psyches, an awareness of each other in the house. We are joined to the beings we love and the ones we cannot bear, to the ones we would kill or give our lives to save.

Gary Eldon Peter is the author of *Oranges*, winner of the Many Voices Project competition, the Gold Medal for LGBT+ fiction in the Independent Publisher Book Awards, and the Midwest Book Award. His most recent book is the novel *The Complicated Calculus (and Cows) of Carl Paulsen*, which won the Acheven Book Prize for Young Adult Fiction. He is a faculty member at the University of Minnesota and lives in Saint Paul.

Start Spreading the News

In the spring of 1996, in my final year of graduate school at Sarah Lawrence College where I was earning my MFA in creative writing, I went to see the Coen brothers film *Fargo* in New York City. It was playing at one of the city's more famous art house theaters in the West Village, and the screen was so dirty that the film's many winter scenes all had a tinge of gray, as if a dust storm had just blown through. I was wrapping up my two-year experiment living on the East Coast, and I'd be returning in a few weeks to my regular life in Minnesota that I'd put on hold to live as a writer.

A few weeks earlier, a man that I'd met at the monthly dance held at the Lesbian and Gay Community Center, as it was then known, asked me to the movie. I'd done very little dating since moving to New York, though on weekend nights I would often take Metro North from Bronxville, where I was living with three housemates, into the city thirty minutes away. I'd wander in and out of the bars in Chelsea and on Christopher Street until the mad dash to Grand Central to catch the last train at 1:30 a.m. back up to Westchester.

I'd relocated from Minneapolis to the East Coast to be a writer and change my life, I'd decided, not for romance. But my time as a New Yorker (albeit one from the suburbs) was quickly flying by, and soon it would be time to rejoin the real world again. So why not make the most of it while I could? I'd likely never have another chance to be a part, even peripherally, of one of the great gay epicenters of the world.

Not long after I started graduate school in the fall of 1994, a man I chatted with occasionally at Splash on W. 17th Street, a bar renowned for its sleek shower décor and equally sleek and muscular go-go dancers and bartenders, told me about the center dances. While there was no romantic connection, we would try to have shouted conversations over the music about the city and my studies at Sarah Lawrence. "I think you'd like it at the center," he said, sipping on a gin and tonic while I nursed one of the three Rolling Rock beers I would ration out during my bar hopping, mindful of my dwindling graduate student bank account. "It's a little a more low key, less . . . *competitive*, I guess you'd say." I wondered if I should take offense, if he was telling me that, in the trendy and fast paced world of the "Chelsea Boys" I was out of my league. But I realized he was likely right. I was in my mid-thirties at the time, having returned to graduate school to focus on my writing after a twelve-year career in the law and in the corporate world, a good ten years older than most of my classmates, and here too, and on the upper end age-wise among the crush of tanned and toned young men who were regular fixtures at the bar.

As much as I might have interpreted and perhaps resented the Splash guy's advice as a comment on my desirability, he was right about the dances at the center. They had a wholesome, high school mixer quality to them. People were friendly and always willing to dance, the floor crowded and vibrant but not stifling, the music loud enough but not so oppressively pounding that you couldn't have a good conversation with someone. And the drinks were a lot cheaper. So while the usual haunts remained on my itinerary, the dances were also a regular event for me, and something that I looked forward to.

My *Fargo* date, Lance, was also a regular attendee at the dances, though we didn't finally meet until I had just a few months to go before I completed and submitted my thesis and I would start making my plans to return home. A graduate of the Yale School of Music, he was the same age as me and a freelance accompanist and vocal coach, a career I imagined to be glamorous, especially in New York City, though he was very blasé about it. "It pays the bills and my student loans," he said, "It's a living." I understood; I had just a few months grace period before mine would come due, and part of me harbored a fantasy that, in all the millions of people who had loans, mine would somewhat get lost in the shuffle, at least long enough for me to get a job and start saving money before Sallie Mae finally caught up with me.

When Lance asked me out for both dinner and the movie, I readily accepted. I'd heard a lot about the film and how it depicted Minnesota, so I wanted to see it, and while it seemed unlikely that much could happen in terms of romance (I'd mentioned when we met that I was leaving New York soon), Lance was easy to talk to and enjoyable to be with, so what was wrong with a friendly date? Over dinner, before the movie, he made it clear that he was in a similar place, having just ended a relationship recently, and wasn't ready for another one just yet. Without the awkwardness of "where is this going to go" questions hanging over us, the conversation flowed freely. He had a subtle but wicked sense of humor, making fun of the overpriced sausage marinara and our indifferent waiter. I felt a twinge of regret that, reassurances aside that we'd keep in touch after I left (we wouldn't), our friendship was likely to be short-lived. Indeed, I'd had similar thoughts about the fate of the other friendships I'd made during my time in New York, and whether this time that I'd taken to be someone else—a writer—would soon seem like it occurred in another lifetime, or had happened to another person entirely.

Even though we'd arrived almost thirty minutes early, we had trouble finding seats together and ended up in the third row, which made the frequent violence in the film even more intense, the landscape which I had grown up in seem even more bleak. But what captured the audience's attention wasn't the gore; it was the way characters talked. People roared at the exaggerated dialect of the heroine, pregnant police chief Marge Gunderson (Frances McDormand), the car salesman villain Jerry Lundegaard (William H. Macy), and that of many of the other characters in the film, their nasal, sing-song speech patterns, the continual stream of "yahs" and "you betchas" and every other stereotypical Minnesotan expression ever uttered. As I sat there watching both the crowd and the film, I felt an odd and unsettling combination of both embarrassment and pride. *A hit movie set in the dead of a Minnesota winter, produced, written, and directed by filmmakers who grew up in my home state!* alongside *Stop laughing! We don't really talk like that!*

But then again, we sort of did. Yes, it was a bit overdone, but at the heart of it, the Coen brothers of St. Louis Park, Minnesota, had pretty much nailed it, at least in terms of some members of my family and others who were part of my growing up. It was a sort of cadence they fell into when they spoke, and while not every sentence necessarily contained a "you betcha" or some other of the stock phrases liberally sprinkled throughout the film, the overall effect was, I had to admit, startingly accurate.

"What did you think?" Lance asked me as we walked out of the theater and into the warm early spring evening. The noise of the city, following the quiet roll of the credits, was jarring. What *did* I think?

"Well, it was certainly different," I replied. *Different.* Another stock Minnesota phrase usually offered when you were asked to give an opinion on something (a work of art, a make of car, a hairstyle, a house color, or really, pretty much anything) or someone and their particular quirks or personality (as in *they're differ-*

ent), but you either didn't know what you thought and wanted to remain noncommittal, or you didn't care for it or them, but you didn't want to seem negative.

"How so?"

"The . . . way everyone in the movie talked."

Lance smiled. "It was pretty funny, wasn't it? With all the blood and gore I guess they thought they should include some comic relief."

"I'm from there. It really isn't like that." The words felt a little hollow, because again, there was some truth to it.

"Well, it's a movie. They probably wanted to heighten it for effect."

"Maybe." I considered asking Lance if I sounded like the characters in the film, but with my Minnesota reserve I decided I didn't know him well enough to have him answer such a personal question, even though it really wasn't all that personal. Or maybe I didn't want to know the answer, because despite all the worldliness I thought I had gained in leaving the Midwest, I was afraid I was still hopelessly Minnesotan.

And besides, it wouldn't have been the first time someone had commented on the way that I talked and reacted, if not with hysterical laughter, then certainly with bemusement. Some of my graduate school classmates, who were mostly from either the West Coast or East Coast, had laughed at my odd use of "go with," as in *I'm headed to the library. Do you want to go with*? To which they'd reply, *What do you mean? Go with where?* That and *soda* versus *pop*. And *in line* (me) or *on line* (them) when we're waiting at the grocery store or at the window at the post office. But it was their reactions to the way my words sounded, which *Fargo* brought into stronger relief for me and which, at least in my mind, set me apart.

Once, during a workshop where a short story of mine had been discussed for the better part of an hour and I spoke more than I had all semester, a classmate made an off-hand remark on the "flatness" of my vowels. I can't exactly remember how the subject even came up (it might have been because we were discussing dialogue in the story I'd submitted for critique). I wasn't sure what they meant until I listened to the vowels of the others, how much "fuller" they were compared to mine.

As I think back on it now, I'm reminded of the scene in *Singin' In The Rain*, one of my favorite movies, where silent film star Lina Lamont, in training for the transition from silent films to talkies, is working with diction coach Phoebe Dinsmore. *Round tones*, Phoebe exhorts Lina in one of their sessions, *round tones*. Lina, unfortunately, is a lost cause with her nasal and grating *can't* instead of *cahn't*. And when it came to my own round tones, and my own Scandinavian flatness, perhaps I was, too.

In the days following the movie, I couldn't stop thinking about my Minnesota self, my New York self, and I brooded about whether all that I had done to change my life to be a writer had also changed anything else about who I was and who I might be in the future. During my time away from the Midwest, I'd had visions of staying and becoming a "real" New Yorker and making a new life in the city, being a new person, someone very much unlike Marge Gunderson, Jerry Lundegaard, and even unlike myself. If popular culture was to be believed, isn't that the reason everyone moved there and why everyone was from somewhere else? At least that was the legend. It's perhaps a little embarrassing to admit, but there were times that Frank Sinatra and "New York, New York" ran through my head at odd times, about making it there, making it anywhere, and all that.

But even if I could never escape my essential Midwestern-*ness*, I had done what I'd set out to do—I'd lived as a writer, and I would soon have a master's degree to show for it. I'd met new people; I'd seen new things. My times in the city weren't just limited to visiting gay bars and leaning against a wall, or sitting on a bar stool, seeing how long I could make one beer last. I went to readings at the 92nd St. Y and at Symphony Space. I bought half price theater tickets to Broadway shows and occasionally splurged for full price if it was something I really wanted to see. I'd also spent long and leisurely afternoons wandering through the Metropolitan Museum of Art and writing in the main reading room of the New York Public Library and, when the weather was nice, sitting on a rock in Central Park, just because I could and I knew I would never be able to do those things again. And along the way, I'd become a New Yorker. Hadn't I?

I'd thought about staying and trying my luck in Manhattan (or Brooklyn, or Queens, or wherever I could find a place to live just so long as it wasn't Westchester). Some of the friends I'd made in graduate school encouraged me to stay as well. *You're a writer. Where else should a writer live except in New York? You belong here!* Though to be honest, in retrospect, that may have been more me than it was them, trying to talk myself into it. And in the end, I didn't really entertain the idea very seriously. In addition to my brand new MFA, I did have a law degree, but I wasn't interested in sitting for another bar exam and another attempt to practice law that I'd already bailed on once, or cobbling together a meager living teaching composition as an adjunct at three different institutions, or working in publishing as someone's assistant, at thirty-six, for $20,000 to $30,000 a year.

I'd also reached my fill of being an illegal renter in a run-down house six blocks from campus, cheap as it was, and the future possible prospect of living with multiple roommates in the farthest reaches of the city was not something I relished. My old job, with health and dental insurance and a decent salary (by Twin Cities standards), and a retirement plan was there if I wanted it, along with my beloved 1990 Honda Civic that I had stored in a barn while I was away, and soon it would be time for me to start paying on my substantial student loans.

But at the core of it, the pull of the Midwest, and home, if not irresistible, was inevitable.

So I made a quick trip home before the end of the semester to find an apartment, called a moving company, used what was left in my savings account to ship everything home to Minnesota, and booked a cheap one way flight on Sun Country Airlines back to Minneapolis, promising myself and the friends I'd made that I'd be back within the year, if not just a few months, for a visit to see whatever plays I wanted for the full ticket price and main floor, center section, to enjoy nice dinners out, and to take cab rides instead of the subway, things I would soon be able to afford to do but that were often out of my reach when I lived there.

In other words, I could have it both ways: part of me would always be a New Yorker, and to borrow from another popular song, no one was going to take that away from me.

It would be seven years before I returned, and two years after 9/11. The weekend of my graduation from Sarah Lawrence, two friends who had flown out to see me get my diploma and I visited the World Trade Center. We took pictures of each other with our disposable cameras standing in front of the iconic Koenig sphere, the familiar horizontal window pattern of the Twin Towers visible in the background. When I visited in 2003, I went to the site and peered through the cyclone fence covered in green mesh that surrounded the hole where the buildings had been, trying to remember what we had seen, what had been there, where exactly we had stood. I tried to imagine what that day in 2001 must have been like, but of course I could not. New York had changed in ways that I likely could not begin to understand or imagine, and everything seemed off balance to me, my sense of familiarity with the city, even the small amount I might have gained on my frequent visits years ago, now gone.

In the end, I was just another tourist, struggling with my Streetwise Manhattan map and the traffic and hordes of people and trying to keep the subway stops straight, even though I'd gotten fairly adept at navigating them during my time in graduate school. The friends that I'd hoped to see were either out of town or otherwise busy, and one classmate who I thought I was particularly close to and who I wanted to surprise with my cameo appearance in New York begged off meeting for a coffee. I tried to shrug off the awkwardness and embarrassment I felt when it took her several minutes to place me and remember that yes, we had indeed gone to Sarah Lawrence together and that I'd once dog-sat for her and her husband in their East Village apartment while they went away for a long weekend.

And I thought about Lance, and the dances and *Fargo* and the theater with its dusty screen, the sticky floor underneath my seat, and whether I should look him up, but then thought the better of it.

It's now been twenty-five years since I first saw *Fargo*, twenty-five years since my experiment in New York. In May 2019, I flew out with my best friend Jim to hear one of my short stories performed and recorded before a live audience for broadcast on a public radio program. If I hadn't exactly made it in New York, realizing that dream, even just for one night, seemed pretty close. Afterwards, we dropped in at the Monster, a gay bar and institution just off Christopher Street famous for its nightly show tune sing alongs. Splash had long since closed, but the Monster was still going strong. I'd spent more than a few nights there as well during my weekend bar crawls, listening to middle aged gay men stand around a grand piano and belt out "Cabaret", "Everything's Coming Up Roses", and, of course, "New York, New York."

Sometimes, rather than hugging the wall as I usually did, I'd move just to the edge of the group surrounding the piano, many of the singers with their arms around each other, some holding hands. But I went no further, not sure if I belonged in the circle, if I would fit in, if I would know all the words, if I could let myself get that close to people I did not know. After I left New York, like everything else about my time there, I thought often about those Monster nights and I regretted that I never joined, never sang, and if I had, if that would have made me one of them. A gay man in New York.

Jim and I toasted my story and the evening, and we toasted New York. A new group was singing the same songs. I wanted to be a part of it, and for that moment at least, I was.

Philippine-born and LA-raised, Elsa Valmidiano is an Ilocana-American essayist and poet whose ancestral roots hail from La Union through her mother and Ilocos Sur through her father. She currently resides in Oakland. She is the author of *We Are No Longer Babaylan*, her debut essay collection from New Rivers Press. Her work has appeared in numerous journals and is widely anthologized. She holds a JD from Syracuse Law and an MFA in Creative Writing from Mills College. Outside of her writing time, Elsa is a legal consultant for a prestigious Bay Area law firm. Elsa is also the founder and operator of The STETosphere, where she offers editorial services for prose manuscripts.

First Home

My father tells me I was almost born in our red jeep. The red jeep stalled on the expressway while my mother was in labor. She had been getting ready for work that morning when contractions began at 7 a.m. Both she and my father worked at the Bureau of Soils in Metro Manila. It would've been my mother's last day at the Planning Department before going on maternity leave.

But I wasn't born in the red jeep. I was born at the closest hospital off the expressway in Parañaque, near where the red jeep stalled. I should've been born at the hospital where my older siblings were born, but my urgency of being delivered into the world would not allow that. The hospital at the nearest expressway exit would have to do. I was born ten minutes after my mother made her way past the hospital doors. By the time I was four, I was madly in love with the color red.

We lived in a two-bedroom home with a large kitchen in the subdivision of Moonwalk on Soyuz Street in the then-municipality of Las Piñas. Las Piñas was not a city yet. Our street was named after a 1960s Soviet rocket. All the street names in our neighborhood had astronautical associations to spacecrafts and rockets from the '60s reflecting the Space Race between the U.S. and the Soviet Union—Apollo, Orbiter, Skynet, Explorer, Mariner, Pioneer, Titan, Luna, Mercury Atlas, Iris, Ranger, Nimbus, and Early Bird. The street names would not sound Filipino at all. America would already colonize my infancy and would embed itself as a purpose, its own Space Race, where you could always race to be better than someone else, or be better than who you thought yourself to be, to the moon and back, or at least just trying to gain passage to the United States of America.

My infant self would already sojourn to Cubao and Project 8 in Quezon City to visit my Lola, aunts, uncles, and countless cousins. I suffered my first car accident with my family at an intersection a block from my Lola's house—my Lola's beautiful house she had built in 1950 after the War, after losing her husband to the War—sold in 2011, torn down in 2012. A multi-story hotel now rests in its place with broken doors and cockroach infestations. My Lola's beautiful house not even an echo of what is presently there.

Between my birth to sixteen months old, my parents never brought me to the home of our ancestors— La Union and Ilocos Sur—as my parents planned and prepared for their final departure from the Motherland.

While they could not bring me to our ancestral barangays Ubbog and Labnig, Ubbog and Labnig were still brought to me—through the sweet coos between my infant self and Lola Ising visiting from Ubbog, and through the sniff-kisses from Lilang Atang visiting from Labnig. Through my grandmothers' hugs and kisses, the land of my ancestors could still embrace me with a final goodbye before we left for good.

Rice paddies, vegetable farms, jeepneys, pedicabs, Mass every Sunday, big family get-togethers, a father working overseas in Sumatra-Kuala Lumpur-Saskatoon-Edmonton-Red Deer-Calgary-Los Angeles, a mother working late nights in Manila with a long commute home, a few yayas, and doting grandparents, were what made Las Piñas home.

Las Piñas was my first home for sixteen months, the home of infant dreams, where memories dissolved before they could materialize into words. Displacement eventually found its way in a restless sixteen-month-old traveling to new places in crowded airports and crowded airplanes. From Honolulu to LAX, my mother would cradle me in her arms, trying to soothe my bloodcurdling screams for five and a half hours without pause. "You were very tired but just couldn't sleep," my mother told me.

Could I have been missing Motherland but just couldn't say in words?

Had my infant self thought it a dirty trick when more than twenty-four hours had passed and we were still on a plane, not yet understanding that we were never returning Home?

In less than ten years after my birth, Las Piñas amidst the Marcos Regime would become something other than Home as surrounding rice paddies and farms would be swallowed by concrete making way for the rapid development of dense new cities that would proliferate at reckless speed.

I cannot tell you what Las Piñas air smelled like before we left—possibly a mixture of campfire, of a pig or goat roasting over an open spit, pink plumerias, sweet mangoes, banana leaves, fresh sun-kissed vegetables from the garden, freshly chopped sitaw under a faucet of cold running water, fresh laundry hanging on a clothesline, and a pot of freshly cooked rice.

I cannot tell you what Las Piñas noises sounded like before we left—possibly the languid rustle of banana leaves in the afternoon breeze, the endless *cock-a-doodle-doo*s from the neighborhood roosters, and the excited staccato Tagalog chatter from small children playing in the street.

Infant memory only presents itself as a hallucination when I have visited the Motherland as an adult, or when I experience small, fleeting moments wherever I have lain my head to rest—Carson, San Diego, Auckland, Dampier, D.C., Syracuse, Quezon City, Tacloban, Lisbon, Tbilisi, and Oakland—when certain smells and sounds become a nostalgic ache for the things I swear I have touched only in my dreams, crushing my infantile amnesia, and rushing through me like déjà vu.

Novelist and essayist Elizabeth Mosier is the author, most recently, of *Excavating Memory: Archaeology and Home* (New Rivers Press). A graduate of Bryn Mawr College and the MFA Program for Writers at Warren Wilson College, she lives and writes near Philadelphia.

In the House of Eternal Return

Something happened that tore open space and time. This is the mystery we're trying to solve, together again as we've tried to be every year since Laurie's divorce.

That time, we landed in Chicago in a raging rainstorm and bailed out Laurie's basement by flashlight after the power failed and the sump pump stopped. By morning, we'd made a myth of our bucket brigade, embellishing the story we'll keep telling forever, like so many other stories we've lived.

The time we scored legal cannabis at the Santé Dispensary in Durango, chanting the menu of childish flavors—Bubbleberry, Chem Brulée, Gelato Cake—as we left the store with a white pharmacy bag stapled shut. The time we drove Colorado's Million Dollar Highway, Frances navigating the narrow road through the gorge as we tried not to see the steep drop with no guardrails. The time we held on for dear life as Frances steered us by moonlight through bear-filled woods on the back of her growling, four-wheeled Bombardier. And after, as we sat on her deck eating ice cream drenched in Kahlua, looking up at the stars, and Frances said, "Will they burn out on their own, or will we cause them to?" The time—the *only* time—I arm-wrestled Frances, my strongest friend, and won.

A kind of homing instinct brings us back together, but it doesn't really matter where we are. Sometimes, we go to Patti's house in California, where we hike through Trabuco Canyon as Frances, a veterinarian's daughter and prize-winning 4H-er, expertly identifies animal droppings along the path. Or we go to Phoenix, our hometown, where my friends know me when my mother forgets my face. At Frances's mountaintop house in New Mexico, we goof around on the challenge course she set up for the Spanish immersion camp she used to run. At my house in Pennsylvania, we trek the loop around Valley Forge, debating names for the real estate agency Frances plans to launch. When we meet again at Patti's house the next year, Frances arrives a day late with a mysterious, persistent cough.

This time, we return to Frances's house, where we wake to the familiar cooing of mourning doves, the soundscape of our childhood spent mostly outdoors. We take a long hike on the Ellis Trail in the Sandia Mountains, and stay up too late talking and playing board games. Frances has lost her taste for the wine we all drink. She takes hits from a tiny pot pipe and tries to teach us to play with different strategies from the ones we learned as kids, like those my brothers used to crush me in their never-ending games of Risk.

Instead of moves meant to combat our opponents, she suggests we try making moves that keep our options open. Try short, simple words in Bananagrams. In Blokus, try placing pieces to extend your reach. It's only fear that makes us fall back on old ways of thinking that don't work, she says, including the belief that winning means someone else has to lose.

Everything is different now and everything is the same.

We are here now and there then: 13 years old, baking on the bleachers at lunch recess, as Frances tells us her dream about the Devil and Jesus wrestling for her soul. I think smoking dill that somebody's brother passed off as weed doesn't call for this kind of biblical showdown. Still, I admire Frances for believing in sin and redemption, as if there were a hidden counter-force to the randomness of our lives in this sprawling desert city laid out in an infinite grid. Is her faith the reason she got high but we didn't, scarfing down chocolate just to chase the pickley taste of being cheated? Frances wasn't faking then, wandering Oak Creek Canyon talking to spirits we couldn't see, and she wasn't kidding now. "I told my parents," she says. "They're going to call your parents tonight."

We all get quiet, so quiet I can hear my new wristwatch ticking as the second hand makes its way around the face. I hear the distant sound of consequences coming, a noise like footsteps on gravel, like a body crashing through the invisible skin stretched between water and air.

***

I am the girl who walked in her sleep. Who once woke up in a strange house, after letting myself in through a neighbor's unlocked door. Who tried to drive our family car—luckily, without the keys. Who would have walked right off a cliff on a camping trip, if my friends hadn't latticed their sleeping bags over mine.

That girl, prone to poetry and daydreams, walks to her high school along a pretty bridle path lined with olive trees. One morning, as I wade through thick fog made by the "winter inversion," cold air trapped under warm like a translucent membrane, a man appears out of nowhere and shoves me to the ground. My schoolbooks fly into the irrigation ditch, crashing with sudden, terrifying truth. In nightmares, I am always mute; but that day, I save myself by screaming. My voice pierces a boundary I hadn't known was body-shaped, mortal, not make-believe. The man runs away, back into the fog. I keep walking, glancing back.

***

In the morning, we hike uphill through Frances's property—past the silent Bombardier that's been put away in the barn; past the empty stable, its door marked by a bear-claw gash; past the ruins of Mijas Camp, with its sun-scorched paint ball court, art building, camp store, and cabins; past Fruitful and Grace, the pine trees we were given to name the last time we were here. Since then, Frances has had to cut back the junipers to let the piñons thrive. But now the piñons are infested with bark beetles, which can fell an old, drought-dry tree in just a few days.

When we reach her shaded *capilla*, I remember the time before this time: how we slipped prayers written on tiny scrolls through the windows of three small bird houses we carried there, cupped in our hands. Frances lit a match and burned a twenty-dollar bill, trying to banish her covetousness. She wants to love the trespassers who cut down trees on this land she knows is hers in deed but God's in trust.

"What's the worst thing that's ever happened to you?" she asks now, as we carefully pick our way back down the mountain, through loose rocks and ankle-high cactus. "Something that reset your life story?"

Laurie and Patti are quiet, pondering the question or just being careful, watching their steps.

I think of the shadow that appeared on my daughter's prenatal ultrasound, which doctors believed was a rare, random form of childhood cancer. Even now, I'm tempted to say that the mass miraculously resolved itself, but the truth is, I can't explain it. The mass was present, apparently not fatal, at her birth. But I was broken, as all parents must be in order to bear both responsibility and powerlessness in this new, uncharted world. I wouldn't wish that revelation on anyone.

"No one gets to tell you that your tragedy is a godsend," I say.

***

I am the girl who once imagined herself grown: sitting at a desk facing a window, writing; a writer. Then, I put words to paper to build a place inside myself where I could live, gripping the pencil so tightly that a callus formed on my right middle finger. Now, the callus—that history—is gone, and I write on a computer in my home office, tapping plastic keys and launching words that land without a sound on a giant screen. As I type, I side-eye the real world outside: the lilac and azalea bushes, the birds nesting in the high branches of the blooming rose arbor, the little gable-roofed playhouse my husband built for our daughters. In the season when I lost my mother, my brother-in-law, and my 9-year-old niece, I scrubbed and repainted and retiled the floor of that playhouse, though our girls are grown and gone. I texted my friends a picture when I'd finished. Seconds later, Frances called me to say, "I see how good that house looks, and I know how bad you feel."

***

In the afternoon, we drive an hour north to Santa Fe, to see the multimedia, interactive art installation created by the Meow Wolf collective. The House of Eternal Return is a Victorian-style house built to scale inside the shell of a former bowling alley, a kind of walk-through science fiction story. The premise is that the house exists in two dimensions: in Mendocino, California, and right here, where we step from the gingerbread-trimmed porch into an ancient, ongoing conflict between chaos and order, between the disappeared Selig-Pastore family and a sinister-sounding organization called The Charter.

There's a framed family portrait over the fireplace mantel in the living room. Fragments of these people's story, potential clues, are scattered everywhere—in diaries, notebooks, and photo albums; in cabinets, closets, and drawers. A young woman dressed in a white lab coat and holding a clipboard informs us that there are no instructions, nor any map to help us understand what happened here. This is an open-ended narrative, she says, that can only be completed in the mind of the viewer. We're free to wander the house, investigate the scene, and put the story together ourselves.

Frances rushes ahead through the dining room, its ceiling eerily rippled where a melted and mangled chandelier hangs. Patti follows slowly, touching the warped chair rail as she takes in the room's wallpaper with its repeating pattern of weird, olive-green trees, like an other-worldly toile. Laurie goes at her own pace, conferring with others, then doubling back to share what she's learned: *The refrigerator is a portal into another dimension!* she tells us. *There's one in the medicine cabinet in the bathroom, and another in the closet under the stairs! Look for the clue in the notebook in the girl's bedroom!*

While my friends explore the space, I anchor myself on the living room couch, diligently reading through materials stacked on the coffee table: the Mendocino newspaper, a day planner, an envelope stuffed with The Charter's agent reports. I learn a few things about the family's backstory. That The Charter keeps tabs on these people they refer to as "a dangerous cabal of Anomaly." That the grandmother's death brought about the family's demise. That the boy in the portrait above the fireplace disappeared while he and his uncle were trying to reach a "fog world" between parallel dimensions.

While I'm busy tattooing my palm with a four-digit code I find in the back of the day planner, betting that these numbers will mean something later, a kid crawls out of the fireplace.

"Whoa," he says, startling me from my solitary study.

For the first time, I see that the hearth is empty, a void with a decorated mantelpiece and family portrait that serve as a symbolic decoy. I leave my research in the living room and follow the boy back through the cold hearth, to an ice cave of colored crystals in the house's secret center. And all at once, I know—I can name—what happened here. This house has been consumed by pain, and this family has abandoned it to search for a new home. There is no one here to tend this fire.

Grief is a house of eternal return, the hub of an immense multiverse, in which all existence has been recurring, is recurring, and will continue to recur an infinite number of times, across infinite time and space. And now we're part of this story, moving through it, trying to plot the unknown. Frances goes first, making up her own rules. Patti moves methodically, relying on her senses. Laurie trusts her intuition. And I'm lost in thought, as I always am, still practicing my dogged, foolish faith in words.

I find Frances in the lobby, shaking pills that are too toxic to touch from a plastic bag into her mouth, quickly washing them down with water to douse the chemical burn. We sit together on this bench, and we sneak out our bedroom windows to roam our neigh-borhood in the middle of the night. We scale our neighbors' stockade fences and cannonball into their swimming pools—waking them, scaring them, pro-voking them to chase us. We run barefoot through pitch-black, glass-filled alleys, dripping chlorine and gulping hot, heavy air. How brave we are, how stupid and safe, breaking curfew and never once get-ting caught.

When I say that we grew up together, I mean that I am home when they are here. Our youth is one con-tinuous summer night, alive with the hiss of cicadas and the pulse of laboring pool pumps, as we wait for something to finally happen to us.

***

This is what will come to mind when Frances texts me a picture from the hospital in Albuquerque, her yellow wristband warning FALL RISK, which I first misread as ALL RISK.

"The yellow band really means *escape risk*," Frances jokes, determined to see every setback as an adventure.

Flight risk, I think, clicking and scrolling through airline websites on the giant screen, searching for flights I will not take, cannot take, during a global pandemic. The *tap-tap-tapping* of my fingers on the keys is a ticking clock, a counter. Or it is a gentle rain striking the window in my peripheral vision, through which the bright moonlight shines.

Outside, in my neighborhood, spotted lanternflies have suddenly appeared. In the late afternoon, I walk and think, *This is new*. Then think again: *Or were they here last year*? Time is slippery now. I recall, or imagine recalling, stories of Philadelphia schoolchildren being trained to kill the invasive insects on sight. Now, the news is only of coronavirus and vaccine trials and schools opening and closing and reopening online, and this picture that might be a memory, of mask-less children joyfully chasing and stomping bugs, already seems impossible. And yet, the omen-insects are here now: dropping from tree branches, catapulting onto cars, baiting me as they bask on the hot sidewalk, lazily spreading their pink, polka-dotted wings to reveal the red lanterns on their bellies. I wince as I lunge at one, then another, launching them without touching them, like tiddlywinks. *Festive*, I think. "Invasive," I say out loud, to no one. This is the word people use as permission to get rid of things, including *this* thing the agriculturalists say will ruin crops and "quality of life." Eventually, I forget to keep a body count of party bugs as I circle the track of this place where I live now, stomping asphalt and concrete to punctuate these endless days spent sheltering in place.

I rise and go to the kitchen for a glass of milk. The house is mine at this hour. I am *dueña de casa*, feeling my way through darkened rooms, falling through space from memory, beyond myself and back into myself: wide awake, grasping the cold metal handle of the fridge. "My friend is dying," I say aloud to the blinding light inside.

I sit down with my milk at my desk, staring at the vast, luminous screen on which the words in my head assemble and dissolve. Behind the screen is wallpaper: a nearly life-sized image of four women, childhood friends, one of whom will leave this world before the others. In this view from a mountaintop in New Mexico, it is always morning. The air is cool and smells of piñon and juniper, and the light falls softly on the shimmering aspens in this place where we are planted, which is to say *home*, our roots twining underground.

Nayt Rundquist is Managing Editor of New Rivers Press and teaches Publishing, Creative Writing, Literature, and Composition courses at Minnesota State University Moorhead. Their writing can be found in *The Citron Review*, *X-R-A-Y Lit Mag*, *Up North Lit*, and others. They live just outside of space and time with their artist-jeweler wife and their fifth-dimensional dogs.

Wandering Greenwood

I drive past an old house of mine, after about eleven years away. In the same way that memory grows fuzzy—incomplete, patchy—this house has gone, blurred, faded. It isn't identical to how it looked when we lived there, but I can't pinpoint exactly what changed. Was our front door always that color? Are those the same bushes we'd had ringing the façade? Had they updated the fence? The house has achieved some temporal state in which it is simultaneously my home and something else entirely. Some homunculus cobbled from pieces of my memories and someone else's childhoods.

There's the backyard where we'd hosted my graduation party: too much sugar and caffeine before racing off to twenty other houses with parties out back and celebrating with friends out until the sun clawed its way up from behind the horizon. Behind that window had been Christmas trees and decorations and presents and the first year my youngest brother was there when I came home from a fall semester. And family visits and arguments and celebrations and just every-days of reading through football games and so many dinners and video games and layers and layers of the tiny moments that accumulate, settle in, coalesce into striations of remembering.

But is that my house? Emotionally, yes; I'll always have a few spindly roots still clinging there, to banisters and doorknobs and chain links. They broke off when I left, parachuting away on the winds to my future wife & future homes & future life. Clinging there, they reach for me, grope, pull me back toward a past I can't return to. Can't touch—but watch and cry and smile and hold them to me as tiny reminders of where I've been.

And driving back out through town is just as strange. Ten years have completely altered it. A post-apocalyptic landscape of entirely alien origins—where the only end-of-the-world was me moving to another state. It's all completely different—all some place that is uncannily a hometown that looks noth-ing like it did when it actually was.

But driving up this 135 that isn't my 135, there are pockets where the gravity is stronger—sink holes that punch through that top layer of unfamiliarity toward what had been my Greenwood a decade ago. There's the Steak 'n Shake where we were the obnoxious teens-then-twenty-somethings that had ordered so much food and laughed so raucously and shout-sang more December-ists songs than anyone needs in a tiny restaurant at two in the morning. And there's the Kroger where we found Lion candy bars and Yorkies, the ones that 'weren't for girls' but the girls bought them anyway. And Eugene bought an entire rotisserie chicken on the way to the drive-in theater and ate it all himself.

And then the flood of emotions wrapped inside each other like Kinder Surprise Eggs. Tripping over themselves to get back to my synapses—from back when hormones and angst made everything a huge, world-ending calamity. To when the future was nothing but a shimmering, bright unknown. To laying on Eric's floor and playing Uno for hours and listening to his newest folk and Indie music. To bonfires at Sarah's house where we celebratorily chucked in that year's homework. To parties at Chris's house, staying up late hopped up on Cherry Pepsi and a hundred tacos for a hundred dollars from Roscoe's. To Smash Bros marathons at Garrett's and Super-Monopoly snow days at Stevie's. To ghost hunting in graveyards. To whirlwinds of times where our lives intersected daily before we all spun out into the adults we're still becoming.

And I nearly cry at the bigness of it all, but it's not sad as much as it's just so much and all jumbled together and loud and bright and wild and wonderful. I wonder what it would be like to go back to then, but it's so big and full of love and beautiful here and now and I can't wait to get back to my wife and the home that we're constructing together—not in backyards and bushes and chain links but in moments of grief and joy and potentialities. Where our roots are twining and digging deep together, strengthened by their hold on each other and clinging to wherever we land.

Elizabeth Searle is the author of five books of fiction—most recently *We Got Him*, from New Rivers Press—as well as the playwright of *Tonya & Nancy: The Rock Opera*, which has been widely produced and drawn national media—and the co-writer of a Feature Film from Duplass Brothers Productions, *I'll Show You Mine*. Elizabeth's previous books include *My Body To You* (Iowa Short Fiction Prize) and *A Four-Sided Bed*, in development for film.

Moving Map

So, where are you from?

This simplest of questions always makes me hesitate. It feels wrong to say PA when I barely remember it. Even more wrong to cite SC or KY when I felt profoundly out of place in both states. And AZ? AZ was and is like another planet to me. Mars, maybe. I think of these states, where I lived only one or two unsettled years, as initials and not full words. When my siblings and I cleared out the sprawling AZ ranch house that had been our loving and beloved parents' final home, an oversized cocoon for their overlong cocktail hours, I didn't want to walk through that house one last time before we made our exit. As with all my childhood houses, the last one never felt, to me, like home.

Where am I from? Where is my "home"?

The long answer: I grew up in four homes and somehow managed to attend four different high schools, my family moving over the span of my childhood from PA to SC to KY to AZ. I left behind, in our quiet Penn Wynn, PA, neighborhood, not only the cozy red-brick house with the pine-needly brick patio—a house that I'd only ever see again in photos, and in dreams—but the girls who played jacks and jump rope with me, who walked with me to and from school. Two girls who might've stayed my "two best friends," Martha and Mindy.

All lost because Hubert Humphrey lost the presidential election to Richard Nixon. On election night in our little brick PA house, my true-blue-Democrat dad, who'd run Humphrey's local effort, knocked over our giant TV in his rage and disappointment, literal sparks flying. *The Hell with it all*, he'd later say he felt about the loss. Impulsively, he took a business job down South and moved his dazed family—my brother and sister and reluctant mom and me—to Home #2.

In rural red-clay-dirt Greenville, SC—the Murder Capital of America; more murders per thousand people than any U.S. city at that time, in the early '70s —we lived in a then-trendy "split-level" house on Route 2. Our tall commanding dad, in his new *the Hell with it all* mode, grew zucchini, and built an elaborate screened porch, and constructed an electric security fence around our acre yard. Our nearest neighbors kept attack dogs in cages. After our beloved tabby cat, Cleo, was mysteriously shot to death on our front lawn (so much for Southern hospitality), my parents bought me two lizards who changed color depending on if they were on the yellow or turquoise mini gravel in their terrarium. They seemed sad on either side. I'd take them out of their plastic terrarium and let them run up and down my arms, their tiny claws scratching without leaving a mark. Wistfully, I named the chameleons Martha and Mindy.

I became a kind of chameleon myself in the years and moves that followed—striving to blend into the rowdy junior high classrooms in Greenville, SC, where the students seemed to speak their own drawling language. I longed to escape to our acre-wide backyard where my sister and I acted out our own "movies" on into my teens. Maybe I'd never have begun writing if we hadn't been isolated in the Carolina countryside, creating our own worlds. But our restless dad left behind Greenville for Home #3 and a job in the bigger, racier city of Louisville, KY.

Dad realized within weeks, he'd admit later, that he'd made a huge mistake in impulsively taking the KY job with little-known Cott Soda Co. (*It's Cott to be Good*). In Louisville, home of mint juleps and my mom's new specialty, Kentucky Derby pie, made with chocolate and bourbon, Mom and Dad both began drinking more heavily: cocktailing away the humid evenings with fellow suburban couples in the crowded cul-de-sacs of Riverbluff Farms.

Neighborhood girls offered me cigarettes as we huddled in a half-built home near our street. But in school, they mocked me and my Yankee accent and my gawky manner behind their lipglossed smiles. At a movie theater, where I worked at the concession stand, the manager patted my ass in my short skirt, giving his smarmy "southern gentleman" smile.

I was glad when Dad announced we were leaving KY; but he was taking another job he'd wind up hating. Which came first, the chicken or the egg? Did my dad drink heavily because he never found a job that suited him, or did he never find the right job because his fine mind was addled by too many nightly bourbons on the rocks? Mom had worried a political career would take Dad from his family. Was Dad's moodiness—I'd worry as Dad sat in his big recliner like Lincoln in his stone chair, brooding with his bourbon—our fault? After abandoning plans to start a hardware business (shrink-wrapped boxes of unused tools for this scheme filled our KY basement), Dad took yet another personnel manager job and moved our family west.

My mother—a high school biology teacher who had to re-start her quest for a master's degree multiple times—made Dad promise this was our last move when we departed on a cross-country trek to Home #4 in AZ, a state full of new arrivals and old retirees.

There was no pretense, as in the South, that these folks were friendly. In that sense, then, I felt a bit more "at home" in the walled-in, eerily quiet suburbs of that desert city.

At the time—the late '70s—it still seemed somewhat unusual to move around a lot. My parents had grown up solidly rooted in PA and Ohio; many in their generation knew their neighbors and maintained longtime hometown friends. Many of the kids I went to school(s) with had known each other since grade school. Others at least felt a familial connection to their region. Maybe an old-fashioned notion. These days, kids who we know toggle between parents who move from job to job. Many form their communities online.

Maybe my generation was, like me, a middle child. While my brother and sister both wound up graduating from high schools that they'd attended several years, my age landed me in four separate high schools (one in SC, two in KY, one in AZ), where I never managed to make friends or make a mark, until my senior year in AZ, when I found my niche with the thespians—the wannabe stars; the fellow chameleons.

I was even cast as the lead in the class play, an apt choice for high-strung teens: *David and Lisa*, set in a mental institution. My character, Lisa, was schizophrenic and only spoke in rhymes. Perfect casting for misfit me. Just when I started feeling at home, senior year ended.

> *"HOME": Definition #1 (so sayeth Google): The place where one lives permanently, especially as a member of a family or household. "I was nineteen when I left home and went to college."*

I was seventeen when *I* left home and went to college—younger than the norm. Maybe my always having been a year young had contributed to my feeling of being lost and awkward through my school years. But like my intrepid dad (by then attempting a new midlife crisis career in AZ real estate) I saw my freshman year at Arizona State University as a chance to reinvent myself. Boldly, I signed up as a theatre major and was "signed on" with a sketchy modeling agency called Plaza3. Walking the fiercely sunny ASU campus baked off my acne and highlighted my brown hair. But I still felt lost at that vast Big Ten University. I got passed over at cattle call-sized auditions for the theatre department plays. Creative Writing 101 threw me a lifeline—a way to keep playing pretend that didn't involve the high anxiety of acting.

By sophomore year, I applied to transfer to Oberlin in Ohio, the one college at that time where you could actually—however impractically—major in creative writing. That was my official reason for wanting to go. The unofficial reason was that I loved the grey-skied campus photos in the Oberlin brochure: intense young music students hauling their cello cases past Gothic stone buildings amidst what looked to be one long rainy day.

My kind of place, I sensed. Though the small college town surrounded by cornfields at first felt isolated and gloomy, I came to find the kindred spirits I'd imagined from those rainy-day catalog photos, including my husband-to-be, an Oberlin alum nine years my senior. Having traded my AZ tan for the pallor of a late-night study denizen, I fell hard for the tall, intense main desk library worker who'd felt so "at home" in Oberlin he'd stayed on after graduating two years before. He worked late; I'd bring him a grapefruit for his break then meet him at 11 p.m., and we'd dance the night away to the Talking Heads and The Police at the college disco.

"Oberlin is the cradle of man, but you can't live in the cradle forever," John quipped as we plotted our escape. Newly engaged, John and I—like many an ambitious pair—flew the Midwest coop and headed east, to the high-crime big-city where John had been accepted in grad school at Yale. We dubbed New Haven "No Haven," huddled together in the railroad-car-sized studio apartment we called Skylab. A good testing ground for marriage, we believed.

I rose at 4 a.m. to take the bus to tend to residents of the New Haven Regional Center for (what was then called) "mental retardation." The bare-bones center was, for the adult residents, their only "home". Earnest young staff like me woke them, helped them dress and brush their teeth, fed them a mass breakfast. We diapered the most helpless, yelled "Male staff!" when the most volatile got out of control: a man once knocking me to the floor. But I stuck it out through John's grad school years. I felt a kinship, especially with the Autistic residents who liked to rock in place and trance out. A thin line, I found, between "artistic" and "autistic." After a wild morning shift at the center, I always felt grateful to return to our spare little Skylab "home".

My new husband was studying away in the newly named field of "Artificial Intelligence" on the outskirts of the grand Yale campus: Manslaw (aka, Manslaughter) Street. Escaping "No Haven" with a new taste for the pleasures of city living, we homed in on—for my own grad school experience—the more manageable New England city of Providence.

We seized the chance to live in the house my great-grandfather had built when he'd arrived off the boat from Ireland to settle in Rhode Island. Great-aunt Molly had just moved to sunny AZ, taking a room in the nursing home near my parents, where her sister, my grandma, lived. Dad's final job was turning out to be caretaker for the elders in our family. Dad took to answering the phone in AZ, "Searle's Geriatrics." As Great Aunt Molly got settled in AZ, John and I moved into her Rhode Island house for two years. We would keep up the two-story saltbox house with its hard-partying upstairs tenants, its double-decker porches and packed attic. Gradually, we'd clear out the house and ready it for an eventual sale.

So, I already had family roots in this frosty part of the country where I was starting to feel—despite my anxiety about entering a high-pressure graduate writing program—at home. Providence combined the quirky historic college-town charm of Oberlin (the Providence streets bearing Puritan names like Benevolent and Hope) with the cool urban allure—and primo pizzerias—of New Haven. During my busy grad school years at Brown, John commuted to New Haven to finish his final class and I worked as a Special Education aide. Our jock tenants upstairs seemed to enjoy nightly sessions of hurling furniture, and our elderly neighbors complained about our own stereo, blasting late-'80s rock. But we had a blast "playing house" in our hundred-year-old newlywed home—maybe the first house I ever loved like a real home.

"HOME": Definition #2; verb: (of an animal) return by instinct to its territory after leaving it. "a dozen geese homing to their summer nest-

ing grounds"; to find and move directly toward
(someone or something) "The missile was hom-
ing in on its target."

Why does one place or another—one house or another—make you feel "at home"? Why do some people
feel settled in one place all their lives, while others travel for most of theirs trying to find—to "home in on"—a
place where they fit in? Why New England for me?

Growing up as a daydreamy bookworm in rural SC and KY, seeking refuge in the school libraries
during recess, I felt aware of a palpable hostility toward nerdy kids like me. No doubt with my 'Northern accent' and bottle-thick glasses and tongue-tied
shyness, I'd seemed strange and stand-offish to those
homegrown Southerners. In New England, as I experienced it in grad school at Brown University, nerdy
students were the norm, bookstores were plentiful,
and the iron-grey days of Rhode Island winters were
perfect for holing up inside, reading, and writing.

Still, we were temporary squatters in Great Aunt
Molly's grandly rundown home.

Gamely, we sorted through Molly's leatherbound
Dickens volumes, inked on the title pages with the
dates—1910 through the 1960s—of each time it had
been read. I did my grad school reading in fusty tweed
armchair, stained under its yellowed lace doily with
my great-grandfather's hair oil. We found envelopes
from the 1920s stored in nightstand drawers, filled
with hair cut from my grandmother's head: gold-
en-brown like mine. The color dulled but unmistak-

able. We shipped back to Molly a 1920s china jewelry box, engraved: *You're witty and you're pretty.*

Then there was the attic, full of empty hat boxes and moldy clothes, where my thrifty great-aunt had hoarded plastic bags within bags, all disintegrating into flimsy, filmy shreds at my touch. We called Junk Men for a final sweep. Heavy-booted men climbed to the attic and threw the remaining detritus of decades down into their open-bed truck while we watched from the emptied living room, shuddering. Would our lives ever be hauled away like this?

But we were young then and focused on the future, on finding our own home. From Providence, we trekked north—"homing in" more deeply to New England—so John could take a software engineer job in Boston. We segued from a cramped but stylish city apartment to a suspiciously low-priced Townhouse-style apartment closer to the suburbs—this became "the place that got broken into" after the day we arrived home to find a big kitchen knife of ours dropped in the living room and a man-sized footprint on our kitchen counter beneath the busted-open window. We spent two years searching for an affordable so-called starter home.

But once we moved in, we dug in. Determined that no kid of ours would be uprooted for repeated moves, we took my real estate developer dad's advice and bought the "smallest house in the biggest neighborhood" that we could find. What made our single-story brick bungalow feel, when I first saw it, like a potential home? Those red bricks.

Driving up to the house with our dogged realtor, I realized maybe I'd been looking all along for the initial home I'd lost back in Penn Wynn, PA: a cozy red-brick house with a red-brick patio. In our house, it's a red-brick *walk*—which became, in the memorable words of our son Will in a high school essay recounting childhood, "the deliciously familiar red-brick walk."

> *"HOME"; definition #3 (is one no one likes to think about): An institution for people needing professional care or supervision; "an old people's home."*

On a wood doorframe inside our longtime home, carefully dated pencil marks chart our son's year-by-year climb toward his dad's six foot plus height. In these same years, my chameleon nature guided me through a writing career that has ranged from fiction to theater to film, much scribbling done in the pre-dawn hours before a day of mothering and teaching and housekeeping. Our house has needed a lot of TLC. Because it was built in the '40s, on a sloping, rocky plot of property, it's been plagued by the usual problems of charming older homes. Water pipes bursting in the basement; our ancient water-boiler heater freezing up in the winters, an aging tree crashing into our roof in a thunderstorm. Our doors stick so they can barely shut in the humid heat; the brick walk we love sags with slick puddles or treacherously frozen ice patches.

These days, with my husband in his sixties and me in my fifties, we tread that brick walk carefully. We joke about needing to repair *our* "crumpling infrastructure"—but we know we are incredibly fortunate to have raised our son, for the last twenty-plus years, in this same old-fashioned house, shaded and half-hidden by our small front yard's huge maple tree.

When the first COVID lockdown order hit in March of 2020, I drove out to over-buy supplies, then—knowing it might be the last time I left home for a while—I slowly pulled into our usual shaded spot in front of the house. I looked up through the windshield at the tree above, those wide-spreading branches that I'd seen daily for decades.

And I thought, *What a beautiful tree.*

Often in the subsequent quarantined year, I would walk outside into our yard, sometimes the furthest we'd dare venture out, and I'd study with newfound fascination our biggest, oldest tree. Amidst the tragic pandemic, we—like other families lucky enough to own a home—were forced to slow down, to sit still, to more fully appreciate those homes where we were, as ordered, "sheltering in place". A home is where you can sit, not move, not want to move on.

My parents eventually came to feel that way about the AZ ranch house where they wound up staying 'til their deaths, staving off the grimly cheerful Desert View Nursing Home where Grandma Searle and Great Aunt Molly both died. In his more relaxed years as an AZ retiree, my dad had the leisure to return to his first love of politics. He ran for State Senate, losing the race but making a name for himself in the Democrat community. We dubbed Dad AZ's "Lone Liberal". The local paper made him a community columnist; he contributed provocative pieces and fiery letters to the editor.

My mother had finally earned her master's degree in her fifties from ASU and found a job that suited her as a children's librarian.

While the vast chillingly air-conditioned AZ house became too hard to maintain for my parents, who increasingly depended on my protective big brother for help, that family-sized ranch house was home to them. I better understand their insistence on staying as John and I begin contemplating our own old age. We too are determined to stay put, at home.

We are home, people say as if they themselves "are" their home. Maybe we say it that way because your home is where you can let down your guard, stop trying to transform into someone else, just be yourself. Many people never reach that place, that peaceful stopping point. Some don't find it until later in life, when we all also start to feel life's limits.

My husband turned sixty-eight in 2020. My son and I were terrified—in the first months of the pandemic—to let him leave the house. Now, as much of the world opens up, John and I still stay close to home, hunkered down in the rapidly aging red-brick house where—if we, like my stubborn parents, can evade that other kind of "home"—we aim to stay. We settled down sooner than many couples, which lends to the illusion we share that we are rooted in place as deeply as our tree. But trees—we learned when one crashed onto our roof—can fall.

Still, for now, for as long as it lasts, we are here. We are home.

Rachel Coyne is a devotee of Pablo Neruda, a collector of vintage editions of Jane Eyre, and a lover of Don Williams songs. She is a graduate of The Perpich Center for Arts, a MN public arts high school, Macalester College, and the Washington College of Law at American University. A long-time resident of Lindstom, MN, her books include *Daughter, Have I Told You?* (Henry Holt), *Whiskey Heart* (New Rivers Press), *Patron Saint of Lost Comfort Lake* (New Rivers Press), and the e-book YA series The Antigone Ravynn Chronicles.

The Only Memoir I Will Ever Write

I'm pretending that you're interviewing me as you read this and that you've asked a difficult question. I never talk about home, so I offer instead—is it okay to tell you a story about someone else's childhood to explain? I'm a writer after all. I only work in stories. Let me tell you about Amantine Lucile Aurore Dupin—George Sand. Her father was an officer in Napoleon's army, and she was traveling with her mother to see him. One night her mother discovers blood on the floor of the inn and wakes the entire house. She's convinced the innkeeper is murdering them one by one in their beds. No one can rest until they follow the trail of blood to where the cook has been honestly butchering a pig or a deer. She and I don't remember which. We were very little. Can you picture her clinging to her mother's side—wide-eyed and frightened? My whole childhood felt like that—the fear of following a blood trail into the night. But also the folly, right? The shame of being so frightened by a lie. A misunderstanding compounded by an overreaction. My whole parents' marriage was a misunderstanding. And because there is a woman in this story, you mustn't think I'm referring to my mother. My father's great sin was selfishness. I've never met a more selfish man. The kind of selfish you only get by being profoundly neglected yourself as a child.

And then there was the setting of my childhood. And there's another memory of George's that explains the whole thing. This is during the war again. Napoleon has defeated Spain and the regiment is housed in a grand palace. This was a time where you could take your whole family to war with you and no one thought to call social services. Her mother has dressed George in a tiny soldier's uniform to amuse her father. Wandering the halls of the seized castle, she finds an enormous mirror. She's never seen a mirror before. She's entranced, dancing before it—not even sure of what she is seeing—not understanding her own reflection. A child in a uniform dancing in an abandoned castle is the America of my childhood—the late '70s and early '80s. That's what it felt like at least. The sound of war always there, lingering in the quiet. The refugee kids—Hmong and Lao—sitting stunned in my first-grade classroom. They don't speak a word of English. Their eyes are dark, haunted French palais. Reagan is the mirror, reflecting us back our darkest selves. How amused we were by his tricks of the light.

This is the only memoir I ever want to write, so I'll end with something actually true. A real memory from my own childhood. I am running home from school up a green hill with two pines—I saw it every day. I still see it perfectly. The sky is very blue with cumulus clouds and I have made a paper kite in class. I can't tell you what grade it was but I am only five or six. The kite is flying behind me as I run, and I am wildly happy. And I think to myself, what a shame that this day is so beautiful and I won't remember it. I won't remember myself or this hill or these trees. But of all those years—that moment of forgetting is what persists.

Tracy Robert, a native of Southern California, has taught writing for nearly four decades. In 2020, her essay, "Losing My Angora Panties," appeared in the anthology *Is It Hot in Here, or Is It Just Me?* (Social Justice Anthologies, Pittsburgh, PA). Her book of linked novellas, *Flashcards and The Curse of Ambrosia*, released in 2015, was winner of the Many Voices Project Prize at New Rivers Press.

Losing the Mother Loathe

I spent a large chunk of my life hating my mother. It was easier to hate her than to support her victimhood, a bottomless discontent I did not want to peer over the edge of or fall into. I felt my hatred kept me safe, and it may well have. My dear sister Amy was pals with my mother and accepted the impossible task of trying to make her happy and stay alive. You could say she devoted her life to my mother's well-being, since Amy never married or had a meaningful relationship outside the closeness to my mother, and four years after our mother died, Amy died by suicide. You could also say hatred saved me from such a fate.

In my sixties, though, the habit of mother loathe became more burden than salvation. I thought breaking the habit would be prescriptive as, say, following a keto diet to lose weight or painting a foul-tasting polish on fingernails to stop biting them. But there is no quick-and-easy regimen for peeling off layers of emotional armor that had grown with my very skin. Luckily, I'd begun to remove them bit by bit in therapy, long before I sensed I was doing so. All I knew then was I was depressed and anxious, and sought to lose those twin afflictions.

Over three decades ago, I made an appointment with a therapist whom friends claimed worked miracles on people like my mother. I did this not for my mother but for my sister, who was worn down from ministering to our mom's problems. When I arrived at 9 a.m. to take her to the therapist, she was dressed and in full makeup, but so drunk she couldn't stand. The neck of a wine jug poked out from under the dust ruffle on her bed. I called Vivian, the therapist, and explained the situation. She said, "Your mother is an alcoholic. But sounds like you could use a session. Why don't you come in, and we can talk?" So began my journey into therapy, which lasted, off and on, throughout two chaotic marriages, over a dozen moves, and my blessedly steady career as an English teacher. Vivian was right about my needing a therapy session—or maybe five hundred.

During my time with her, I learned how to release anger by thwacking a tennis racket or towel on a mattress and yelling, "How dare you!" I learned to allow myself to cry when I was sad, after years of burying my sorrows in achievement and stoicism. I learned it was not normal for a mother to trundle into the living room in her bra and panties and kneel at the feet of my high school boyfriend, admonishing him to treat me better than my father treated her. Nor was it normal for a mother to threaten suicide if my sister, age thirty, moved out as planned. I learned I was a textbook adult child of an alcoholic, having married two addicts in succession, and blaming myself somehow for their compulsions. I learned to break an unspoken rule at least once a week, whether that meant wearing unmatched earrings, or getting a second divorce (oh, the shame!), or taking a leave of absence from teaching in order to write.

Therapy permitted me to seek and live a more fulfilling life. But I still hated my mother. I continued to hate her even after her death, because her dependence on my sister was psychic enslavement, and perhaps led to her suicide. I felt righteously justified in holding onto my hatred, as if doing so honored my sister.

When you hate your mother, it's like dipping your drinking cup into a toxic pond. A mother is as essential to life as water, and by hating her I poisoned myself—while also protecting myself—for a long while. My hatred was much like a vaccination, injecting a potentially harmful substance to defend against a more harmful substance. In this case, the more harmful substance was my mother's despair. I felt it was contagious. My sister's life and death could well be indicative of its contagion.

But here I was, an old woman, who no longer wanted to bear the heaviness of mother loathe. A mother is everyone's first home, and I definitely needed to get my house in order and rid myself of antipathy for where I came from. I turned to my only close living relative, my brother, for help. After all, he'd been the person, several years back, to ask, "Why expend energy on hating a dead person?" Yet Matt had no solutions but further therapy, and I frankly was therapied-out. I believe deeply in the transformative powers of therapy: it is the reason I identified my hatred as a burden. "Naming it is claiming it," as they say in therapy circles. Fair enough. I claimed it. The hatred, though, still seemed attached to me, like a tumor requiring removal. So far as I know, there is no surgical procedure for excising destructive emotion.

Matt's wife Cathy, however, had a suggestion. A few years back, a colleague who'd been her friend and professional ally, turned against her. She had no idea why he changed so quickly and completely, and the betrayal hurt and enraged her, then settled into a generalized hatred. Gradually, Cathy wearied of lugging that hatred around. She and my brother attended a yoga workshop in Tuscany where they met another attendee—a therapist, ironically enough—who taught Cathy an effective pose and technique for releasing hate, and she subsequently instructed me.

Basically, you invent a mantra that addresses the person for whom you bear the hatred, then settle yourself in a chair. You cross your ankles, right foot over left, and cross your wrists, left hand over right, clasping your hands between your thighs. You close your eyes, recite the mantra in your mind, and sit with it for a moment, breathing. That's all.

It doesn't sound like much, but it let my sister-in-law get over the stubborn hostility the betrayal had produced in her, and she's an intelligent, no-nonsense person. I trust her. I also figured since I was dealing with a mother and not a co-worker, I'd need to use the regimen more than once to produce the desired result. I determined I'd practice it several times in a month and see what happened.

I won't reveal my mantra because I'm superstitious that a mantra loses its power if you give it away. I will say it expressed gratitude to my mother for bringing me into the world, and set her free from the prison of hate I'd long held her in. Those are not the precise words I used, but after assuming the chair pose and repeating my mantra a few times, I began to experience a love for my mother I hadn't felt for years, so unfamiliar and welcome it made me weep.

I also began to recall specific pleasant memories of my mother. She read books to us several nights a week, and our favorite was *The Tall Book of Make Believe*, an anthology of stories and poems, illustrated by Garth Williams. We particularly liked a tale called "Bad Mousie", which chronicled the misdeeds of a rodent who was loved by a little girl named Donnica. Her mother tried to rid the house of Bad Mousie by sweeping him out the door with a broom or tying him to a fence post for the night owl to eat, but he always managed to make a comeback.

My mother's frequent warning, when any of her children crayoned the wall or carved wooden furniture with a penknife or sassed her, was, "Don't be a Bad Mousie!"

The warning ended when we were teens. I was the only child angry and undetached enough to sass her by then, and she drunkenly smacked my face for it once or twice. I've felt the sting of those smacks for years, yet now, the sting is tempered by my remembrance of Bad Mousie.

I also recollected that every summer before the start of school, my mother took me shopping at Topanga Plaza. A former model, she knew how to put together fashion ensembles. She taught me to wear clothing that accentuated my small waist and didn't run too tight around my ample butt. We visited our choice clothing shops, Judy's and Contempo Casuals, and Leed's for shoes. If we really splurged, we'd visit the department store, Joseph Magnin. She bought my first pair of heels there, red patent leather with a square toe and chunk heel, a silver pilgrim buckle at the vamp. I recall a dress from Judy's because I wore it for good luck when I won the seventh grade spelling bee. It was black and white polka-dotted cotton, puffed-sleeved, with a hot pink grosgrain ribbon tie at the empire waist.

She bequeathed me a sense of style I still delight in. No more puffed sleeves or pilgrim shoes, but I do see clothing myself as an art, especially with an aging body that presents certain aesthetic challenges.

In the middle of our school clothes shopping day, we took a break to have lunch at the Jolly Roger, a pirate-themed restaurant. We were a strictly middle-class family, and while we sometimes had dinner at a local Mexican eatery, we hardly ever went out for lunch. My stomach was somewhat growly with anticipation as I read the menu, because of the rareness of the occasion. My mother ordered the Shrimp Louie salad without fail, and I either went for the Reuben sandwich or a teriyaki burger.

I can fully reenter the decadent thrill, there in a Jolly Roger booth, how close to her I felt, and special, and momentarily forget the dramatic shatter that awaited our family.

Another memory came to me recently as I was taking a walk. I thought about the music my mother introduced us to through the albums she played on her hi-fi, great music by Ella Fitzgerald, Lena Horne, the Kingston Trio, Broadway musical soundtracks, Leonard Bernstein's *Classical Music for Children* series, even Mitch Miller's sing-alongs. And Sinatra. Of course, Sinatra. As I walked, I started to hum a song, one that my mother used to sing with us, joyously, and we requested she play it again and again.

The song was "High Hopes," which won the Oscar for Best Original Song for composer Jimmy Van Heusen and lyricist Sammy Cahn at the 32nd Academy Awards.

> Once there was a silly old ram
> Thought he'd punch a hole in a dam
> No one could make that ram, scram
> He kept buttin' that dam
>
> 'Cause he had high hopes
> He had high hopes
> He had high apple pie
> In the sky hopes

The song and its words took me back to my childhood living room with my siblings and mother, all of us alive and cheerful and singing, and I thought, *What a fabulous song to teach children.* I loved the playful use of language and the upbeat message, and as I continued to hum it, I began to sob on a public sidewalk. Luckily a pandemic mask covered half my face, and I was wearing sunglasses.

These memories may seem like trivial bits of nostalgia to others, but after not being able to retrieve them for decades, to me they're nothing short of phenomenal.

I'm aware that years in therapy did much of the heavy lifting as I learned about myself and the way my family of origin shaped and misshaped me. I give myself and my therapist credit for that. I'm also aware that the technique my sister-in-law showed me might be a trick, since the desire to lose the mother loathe was already in me. But even if it was a trick, I'll endorse it because the trick worked.

For decades, the ill will I bore my mother blocked up any loving feelings I had for her. I absolutely could not allow myself to have them. Curiously enough, the person I hated made the memories that led me to love her again. She in fact gave me the tools with which I conquered hatred, but I couldn't get to them until I lightened up on hating her. How frighteningly simple yet complicated that concept is, all at once.

While I will never perform the miracle of making my mother happy and whole, I have performed the miracle of remembering her in a happy light.

Oops, there goes a billion kilowatt dam.

A DIY Trip Back Home, Minimal Travel Required

Out of the blue, ask someone—anyone—if they're happy. Inhabit the pause that occurs after the simple question. Look into a jewelry case you haven't opened in years. Try to untangle the knot of fine chains. Wonder how chains become tangled by nothing but time in an untouched case. Remember a time you loved your mother and also a time you hated her. How is that possible? Ask, too, how it is that your mother hated the giggling, storytelling, cookie-baking woman who was your grandmother and her mother. Think about contranyms like *cleave* or *bound* or *sanction*. Account for why we speak a language that trifles with our intelligence. Watch your ancient dog gallop in sleep dreams then struggle to walk when he wakes. Describe a nonbinary gender to your father in twenty-five words or less. Collect extra points if he responds without profanity. Ponder why home is solace to one person and torment to another. Now ask yourself whether you are happy. Inhabit that pause for the rest of your life.

J.C. Mehta is an Aniyunwiya (citizen of the Cherokee Nation) writer, artist, and storyteller. They are the author of over one dozen books and the recipient of numerous fellowships and residencies, including a US Fulbright Scholar Award. Learn more at www.thischerokeerose.com.

Excerpt from *American Baby*

"Last chance for Coca Light." I looked away as England was disappearing below me. In the middle seat, his legs were splayed open like a child's. Even after all these years together, I hadn't settled into that comfortable kind of familiarity with him like everyone says you're supposed to.

I nodded at the flight attendant as she ambled her little cart down the narrow aisle. After a year in London—in that tiny closet of an apartment in South Kensington where we shared a bathroom with the rest of the basement flats, yet somehow never saw any of our neighbors' faces—it still didn't feel like long enough. It had been easy to pretend. To spend my weekdays on the Tube, hunkered down in that little desk at the entryway to the fellowship office helping Brits desperate to be anywhere but on this island, desperate to get full-rides to America. *Don't you know how good you have it?*

"Did you talk to Susan and Gary today?" he asked. Dan took his own soda from the attendant, his bit-ten-down nails already sweating with the condensation. I had always hated those hands. Still couldn't fathom why I let them inside me.

"I emailed them last night," I said. The European version of Diet Coke sizzled against the cup too full of ice. "They'll be at the international arrivals for us. You don't think it's weird?"

"What?" he asked, while slouched over the *Dungeons and Dragons* book propped on the shaky little airplane table.

"You know. Like, living with my ex's mom and stepdad."

"We're not *living* with them," he said. "It's just for a couple weeks, until something comes through. We applied for about twenty jobs, something will happen. And they're not just your ex's parents. They're your adoptive parents."

"They just adopted me so I could be on their health insurance," I said under my breath.

"You know what I mean. Why would it be weird?"

But it was weird. It had been six years since I'd broken up with Susan's son, who'd since been married, divorced, and was now dating another girl with the same name as his ex-wife. They no longer lived in the house I knew when I'd been a child, scraped out of the car I was living in at fifteen and saved—secured their martyrdom nice and tight.

The ride in their white Escalade with the camel-colored seats was filled with Gary's voice that toed the line between booming and nasal. Every five minutes, Susan would crane her neck around. "Make sure those suitcases aren't moving," she said. "This leather was imported from Germany."

"Yeah, yeah," I'd say. Of course it was. Everything was imported from Germany, the country Gary clung to even though he'd been born and awkwardly raised by an ex-Nazi sympathizer in Queens.

"Here we are!" Gary said grandly as we pulled up to their hilltop home on the outskirts of Lake Oswego. The Oregon wilderness opened up in the valley below, and the too-young pines that hugged their garage shook as the doors opened. "Did Susan tell you we upgraded the theater room? We can watch the new James Bond tonight, I have the director's cut—"

"They're probably *tired*, honey," Susan said. For once I was grateful. Maybe she had saved me after all. "You know Angela's old room?" she asked as the Escalade stopped purring.

"By the atrium? Yeah," I said. It had never been Angela's room. Susan's daughter hadn't had a real room in her mom's house since, well, ever. The reason probably being that she'd chosen her dad to live with at five years old, I guess.

"You two can stay in there. Take the bags through the main entry. I don't want them scraping the hardwood."

As Dan and I lifted the stained suitcases out of the back, the only evidence that I'd spent a year abroad was the tired tags from Heathrow. They could have been anybody's.

"Angela's old room" held perfectly matching oak, blonde furniture that was too heavy. The queen bed was shoved between two windows and drowning in a Laura Ashley floral pattern, flanked on either side by tables on steady legs. Only about two feet in the closet had been cleared out, but that didn't matter. Why bother unpacking, anyway?

"We should go be social," Dan said. I watched him as he leaned down and pulled out the same sweatshirt he wore every single day. Pulled on the Fossil watch that he thought was so clever because, hey, he was from Fossil after all.

"I'm tired," I said. "They won't be offended."

"Gary will be offended." Dan squared off towards me. Even when he pulled himself up to his full height, he was barely as tall as me. *Why did the short ones always like me?* It had always been like that. When I was young—or at least younger than twenty-six—I told myself they were cute. I didn't realize what I really meant was non-threatening.

Why do you think you know them better than me? But, "Okay," was what came out of my mouth.

Still smelling of plane, we dragged ourselves into the kitchen and hunkered down on the leather barstools. Susan busied herself at the sink, deadheading the lucky orchids that were allowed to call this massive room home instead of the greenhouse on the wrap-around deck. When I poured some water and set the glistening crystal on the marble countertop, she let out a small sigh as she bustled around the kitchen and wiped up the single drop that had spilled onto the white slab.

Is this how all gold diggers end up?

Five weeks had never seemed so long. Dan could hide away most of the day at a short-term software design gig he'd lined up, but me? I had nothing. The itch got so bad—with Susan following me around like a dog digging up any crumb trailed behind, and telling the story *daily* of how, when I was sixteen, I'd accidentally swiped red nail polish on her carpet—that even Central Point sounded good.

"You're going to go see your mom?" Dan asked, incredulous. "Is that . . . a good idea?"

I glared at him over the book. I'd been stuck reading the same paragraph for five minutes. "I'm going crazy here," I said.

"And you don't think that'll make it worse?"

He had a point, I had to admit that. Even as he kissed me goodbye at the Greyhound Station and I willed myself not to wipe the remnants of his saliva off my lips until I turned away from him.

It took four years after she'd kicked me out at fifteen to speak to her again. Then, it was just because my dad had died at the Indian Hospital in Oklahoma and, well, death can make you do things. For the past six years, I'd been unable to be around her for more than three days before another fallout happened.

Two days. Going down to stay with her two days should be safe. I leaned my head against the grimy bus window and watched the signs on I-5 count downward. By the time the thirty-minute break at McDonald's rolled around, I knew it was a mistake.

"Ray's here," my mom had said when I'd called and told her about coming.

"Who?"

"Ray? You know, the guy I told you about."

"The handyman?"

"Well, yeah. He's staying out in the bar."

"Why?" My mom had housed a menagerie of people at "the bar" over the years, starting with Susan's son when he'd run away from Portland at eighteen to be with me. Before she kicked me out. Then it was any stray who rambled along.

"Oh, you know. There's a lot to be done."

"But why's he living there?"

"He's not *living* here, Jessica," she said. I could hear the shrill in her voice start to flap to life.

"Staying there, whatever. How come?"

My mom sighed. Even in the crackling pay phone, while I watched my bus mates tuck into dry burgers through the restaurant windows, I could hear her hatred of me. "There's just a lot to do here. Okay?"

"Like what? What's he done so far?"

"I don't *know*, Jessica. Alright? Oh, and don't forget to get off at the gas station in Central Point. I don't know why I should have to go all the way into Medford to pick you up."

I'd heard about Ray, of course. Every month in London when I made my obligatory call, he crept into the conversations more and more. "I think he's a meth addict," my mom had said once, bluntly. I'd still been dizzy with the whiskey and Coca Lights from the daily after-work pub outing.

"Then why are you still having him around?"

"Was," my mom had said quickly.

"All right?"

But when I dragged my backpack off the bus at the gas station in Central Point under the guise of going to the bathroom and saw the two of them standing there, he didn't look like a meth head. He looked like every other fifty-something guy in that suck of a town who'd never gotten out.

"Hi," I said awkwardly, grateful to have the straps of my backpack to hold onto. Why would she bring this guy to pick me up?

"Your mom's told me all about you," he said as she swooped in for a hug. I hated her hugs, always had. I couldn't help but stiffen to get my way through it.

"I'm sure she has."

"London!" he said. Ray picked up his greasy hat to run oil-stained fingers through dirty hair. "I've never been outside the West Coast. 'Cept for Vietnam, of course."

"Of course," I said. I heard the haughtiness in my voice, but couldn't swallow it back up. London was the first time I'd ever left the country, and even then it had been for an internship to finish my second year of grad school. Still, I'd jammed as many extra countries into that year as I could. Spain, Scotland, France, Denmark—anything except Germany. And Italy, which we'd called off when we realized we were broke and tired.

"How's Dan?" my mom asked.

"Fine."

The five-minute ride to the little white stucco house I grew up in was the kind of quiet reserved for dead things. "How's Erin?" my mom asked. She sat in the passenger seat for some strange reason while Ray angled the Nissan towards home.

"She's good."

"She still in Alabama?"

"Georgia," I corrected. I'd been correcting her about that for two years.

"Jessica's best friend is going to be a doctor," my mom said to Ray. That was surprising, that she'd brag about anyone except me.

"That so?"

"She's getting her doctorate in math education," I said. "Not, like, an MD."

"God, can you imagine? A doctorate in math—"

"Math *education*," I corrected.

"Didn't you have to beg for that D- in math for stupid people freshman year?" my mom asked.

I felt my heart freeze and felt Ray's eyes in the rearview mirror.

"I don't like math," I said.

"Well. I think the feeling's mutual," my mom said. The tires chewed through the gravel in her driveway.

Every time I came here, it was smaller. That happened, of course, I knew that, but this small? I couldn't bear it. Funny how the smell of childhood knocks you back. Foreign things were peppered around the tiny front room. Ray's flannel shirt draped across the cracked vinyl loveseat. Ray's empty beer bottle resting on the knockoff mahogany desk that held up the beast of a desktop—the same computer I'd found my father's emails to some woman up in Scio that broke up the entire family over a decade ago. Ray's smell mixing with the cloying hazel-nut air fresheners plugged into the wall.

"So!" Ray said as he settled into the couch like he belonged there. "What's next? Your mom said you're staying with . . ."

"Susan and Gary," I said. It sounded stupid; he wouldn't know who they were. But I didn't know what else to call them.

"They're family friends," my mom said as she emerged from the kitchen. Ice shook like scared children in her large plastic cup filled to the brim with brown soda. It got lighter every time I saw her, the vodka taking up well over half the cup by now.

"Nice, nice," Ray said.

"I mean, we're just staying with them a couple weeks until we figure something out." I hadn't told her anything about the job applications overseas, and I sure as hell wasn't going to until anything was confirmed.

"I know how it is to be in between things," Ray said. I kept expecting him to check me out, sneak a look at my thighs or will my neckline to sink lower. My mom turned on the television, so loud that nobody but her could talk or think.

"Your hair's blonder," she told me. Self-consciously, I touched it.

"Yeah," I said.

"Why don't you do it that way you did before? The blonde on top and brown underneath . . ."

Because I don't live to suit you. "That style is super outdated," I said. She sniffed. I couldn't tell if it stung her or not.

"Welp, I better head out back," Ray said. "I want to try and get that fence repair done."

My mom huffed, the sound a petulant kindergartner would make. "Aren't you forgetting something?" she asked and stuck out her bottom lip. At sixty years old, it veered farther into fucked up, senile territory than anything close to flirting. But still, Ray bent down and pecked her on the lips.

"Can I check my email?" I asked as he folded his long frame upward.

I angled my body so it perfectly blocked my mom's view of my email. Not that she could have read that far away, anyhow. And it was like it was meant to be. Sitting there in my inbox was an email from Gangnam Language Program with the subject line, "Welcome, new teacher!"

My heart pounded as I opened the email and scanned the offer. A start date in three weeks, just over $2,000 per month, free airfare, and a free apartment. In particular, the school director wrote, "I am especially joyful that you will join us as a couple. We have found that couples acclimate more quickly to life in Korea." It was signed "Miss Choi," and included a photo of smiling children gathered before a table with a veritable jungle of fruits before them.

The back screen door slammed. "Ree!" Ray called. "I need your help with somethin'."

I turned to my mom. "Dan and I are moving to Korea."

"Where's that?" she asked and took another long pull of the whiskey-Coke as Maury Povich's audience went wild on the screen.

"You know, Korea? Like, Asia."

"What the hell are you talking about?" she asked. Ray appeared in the arched doorway.

"I mean, we've been applying for teaching jobs overseas, and we just got the acceptance letter."

My mom stood up and stormed out. Ray raised his bushy eyebrows at me and followed her. The screen door slammed twice more, and I could hear her raging voice on the back patio.

I inched down the short hallway, past the kitchen painted a Halloween orange, and pressed myself against the wall. All the way until I was fifteen years old, even though the height hadn't changed in four years, my mom had made me stand dutifully on my birthday as she pressed in permanent ink the date and my height on the wall. How I'd shrunk since then, I don't know. But I stared at those dates as I let their voices carry in to me.

My mom sobbed, as she always did. It was so common it hadn't meant anything to me in a lifetime.

"You need to pull it together," I heard Ray say quietly. His voice was firm. "You go in there, and tell your daughter congratulations."

By the time I'd slipped back into the living room and fixed my eyes on Maury, by the time I heard the screen door gently open, I'd already made up my mind and emailed Miss Choi back. And wondered if I could swap my bus ticket for a return trip that same evening. Wondered if I could will yet another country to feel something like home.

Natanya Ann Pulley is a Diné writer (Kinyaa'áani & Táchii'nii) and she is a recipient of a National Endowment for the Arts 2022 Creative Writing Fellowship. Natanya is the founding editor of *Hairstreak Butterfly Review* and is an Associate Professor in Fiction and Native American Literature at Colorado College. Her debut story collection *With Teeth* was published by New Rivers Press (Oct. 2019), and she lives in Colorado Springs, Colorado.

No Trespassing

It was disappointing for you. You asked to see a photo of my mother's mother's home. Shima suna's hogan. You were thinking of the sparseness, the smallness, the singular room without electricity and plumbing, and how this "home" to you should be shown to others. You crave looking at a photo of so little, to shake your head and think, "Oh my." And to find all the ways your own home and mine and my mother's have improved. Very little has prepared me for this moment, when I'm asked to show off (or show down?) the home of my mother's as if to say she came from there (from nothing) and now her daughter is here and isn't that something? Isn't that progress?

But I bring to you, instead, views from the mesa above with the hogan and corral nestled among the reds and blush and sage of the desert. I bring photos taken directly in front of the hogan of family, of puppies, of the sun setting in the back. I bring photos taken from the door of the hogan to the east, a sun greeting. The grain of wood against a blue sky. Small cactus. A chicken. And my brother's young child leaning through the corral's slats to give a lamb a kiss.

I don't bring them all at once. I look through a photobook and come back to our family room with one. You look at it and shake your head. You want to show the other guests (your family) the smallness and the emptiness and the flatness you see. I make you say it over and over. "No, not this one. The one your mother posted. The small house in the middle of nowhere."

I do not bring you the poverty porn you seek, the poor Indian testimony you want of this land and me. I say "Oh! Yes, I'll go find it!" and trickster back with everything but and do not explain why.

But dear one, please know: your dissatisfaction and frustration are gifts I build for us both. I am funning, yes. But I am also making space for you to see me—a mother's daughter, a grandmother's blood, a clan of mothers stretching wide and forever—in front of you with photos of life and not our death. Of life and land loved.

Beaudelaine Pierre is a journalist, scholar, and novelist who writes about her native Haiti and her adopted Youwès. She is the author of *You May Have the Suitcase Now* (New Rivers Press, 2021), and the co-editor of *How to Write an Earthquake / Comment écrire et quoi écrire / Mou pou 12 Janvye* (AHB, 2011).

Se pase m ap pase

Se pase m ap pase
Mwen pa vin pou m rete
ni kanpe tant mwen
byen fon nan kè w
ni chanje devan pòt ou, oswa
revolisyone w
Se pase m ap pase
Tou dousman
Ni ou ni mwen
nou pa menm moun nan ankò
nou pa rann nou kont
Se pase m ap pase.

I am in passing, only

I am in passing
and nothing more.
I am not here to stay
nor plant my tent
deep in your heart
nor change your house front
or make a revolution.
I am only in passing, and
quietly.
And you and I
are no longer the same
and we don't feel the change;
I am in passing, only.

I Live Under TPS

I.

It was my mother's land, it is mine now, I know it's yours. When I say *the land* in a language that is not home, I bite the tongue in my mouth as if the tongue in my mouth is not my tongue. I can never have too much ground to keep me standing, but can I promise not to stand my ground longer than necessary. It was Louverture whose boots wore down the intestines of nineteenth and early twentieth centuries, and the lingerie lines of the twenty-first century era are, as far as we know, an unbounded sky. Every now and then the genetic materials of a Hollywoodian prokaryote are coded Made in Nollywood; we wonder why the roots run so deep, so infinite. (But) In no wonder, the modern citizen takes a seat in analogical safeties. For as far as biocitizenry is concerned, she is, naturally, the situation of her story, her beginnings her ends, fully total, fully self-image, fully tamed.

I knew nothing of home until, as a child, I watched my mother leave the native land. Over the years, home has become palpable, in transit, in dislocation, in the folds of time. So that to conjure (my) ground, I reach for a language released before it reaches the mother tongue where it will have gone after it has left to become mine right in the moment it leaps to cut through you. Does where I appear to be (projection, image) rotate according to prefigured analogies or from being off of my situationstory? Or is it that I am the infinite play of your own showing? There are old taste buds minted into fresh ones; new languages standing on the back of old barracks; borrowed lungs that manufacture themselves in dislocation, in slit, beyond all beyonds. It is possible to conceive the tongue in my mouth as not my tongue.

From Latin *natura*, nature says: the course of a thing; and from another nature course, a thing taken from its root *nasci*, so that to be born Haitian, for instance, is to innately possess the integer of the *genea*. But what is the *genea* if not a lure, a measurement (an observer who observes herself observing herself, unaware she is (in) the *situationstory*), or at best a diffraction: the image of a thing as not the thing in itself, the thing in itself in decomposition, in vivo, in trans, in void, off, in lost to be found? A biped as opposed to a crustacean or a plant, but a crustacean and a plant and a biped altogether; being here and from this and not from that and in this way and in that other way. Simply-humans in manageable bits, expectant, and just there, blank, from nature to culture to sociality to human samples differentially coded from a certain elsewhere, there, outside of the scope of measurement, neither I nor you, neither this nor that.

And here I stand in the semidarkness end of your skyline. Occasionally, I am the enchanted newcomer catching up wonders in the singularity of holes. Now and again (more like your ends and your edges), I am sequentially clustered into profitables, analogies, and memberships. Almost all the time, you're either on one or the other side of your orbit, unlike Marie who says she doesn't speak any world languages but her serotonin. I necessarily abide in you. (But the two of you) Yourself and the radius of your circumpolar zone, operate like a world of its own out of the sun's glare. You've never felt a thing, fully footed you are in the dark end of your own blackness, uncovering what it feels like to unglue yourself from your own image. Isn't it like seeing yourself dead?

I live under TPS. First in the basement of 1693 Charles Avenue, then in a two-bedroom in the Highland Park neighborhood, and then in the column of the Federal Register in what feels like forever. It's impossible not to see myself exceeding the borderlines of my planetarials. I am under Temporary Protected Status; (in) a shithole; what nature (*genea*) is there to see here? Utter darkness. The bones of time I hold (still) inside my chest to make time feel wanted. What I thought was your tongue turned out to be my homeland.

II.

Once or twice a year, in the Saint-Michel Rue Guerrier barrack, workers from Kanada sit around bowls of rice cooked in lards and *pwa congo sèch*. Auntie Fito lives in Miyami. Eslie is in Port-au-Prince doing secondary school. Anytime soon, Tonton Fito will trade his aura of the metropole against a Saint-Michel *poul mannin*. I will go to Port-au-Prince after my *sètifika* to become a journalist or a lawyer like Tonton Fito who practices both and roams between Miyami and Port-au-Prince and Saint-Michel. From my dad's corner, it's a matter of *poul mannin*, contentment and enjoyment, of time working, of putting time in its realm of relative progression, to see a grain of mustard as wide as a fold of the sky; to come out of *lethargia*. The bougainvillea treats its spines as climbing aides, and the river in its naturalness will let go of its dreams. As a child, I lived the world beyond the shortness of my image relation. Myself, in part and in whole, is the most difficult thing to get hold of, having worked through *lèt sinistre*, OEA, and Le Cid, we put clothes on in the classroom, just so we get to Molière and Racine. Fine, the spirit inhabits the mind, which find holds in the body here and not there in exclusivity; and I was in the past, as I am now present, in the future in which I live. Is it that to nature is to ceaselessly perform an act of gravity? But (and this is the point), who gets to pack my selves, hand them to me, say, *Here this is home*?

A near-death precipice from which you're pulled back, unaware, unaware; a *goudougoudou* opening up the patterns of family lineages beyond circumferential stardomes; how can you know for sure the blow makes up the name; (or) shall we say that the name makes up the blow, how can you tell; Haitians get to record thousands of different names for earthquake; a blow in English, another in Ayisyen, and another and so many *genea* lines at fault; a 4:50 p.m. Tuesday afternoon, accommodating in its radius uneven grounds, walking feet, and its strangeness of not being like any other; a near death passage and the awareness that cancels out the slit of death; a name listed in the missing person report for an earthquake they split; a house un-holding the tremor of its undoing to forfeit itself into symmetrical analogies; blows in the shape of everyday coffee mugs—how you know you're under protection, the moment you notice you're guarded against yourself, times in reverse making normalcy alien in the orbit of holes mutating their radius. It's difficult to say where home begins or whether August 14, 1791, lies in full with August 14, 2021; that a *tremblement de terre* doesn't line up with its quakes is not the reason we're here for, of course; the buried is brought back to life by a miracle of some sort, not fully realizing their totalizing, slowly coming to terms with its terrors, sometimes wondering if (surviving) the blow was worth its faults, and almost all the time wishing she wasn't performing a show coded together before she entered the image-repertoire of a Napoleonic ensemble.

Williams says of "nature" as being one of the most complex worlds in the English language; in that, to nature is to witness *Clitandre* achieving embodiment in *Dézafi*, I mean *Fresh Girl*, the inherent forces, irrecoverable for the most part, which makes me an abstract within the borderline order. I then suppose, homing myself entails seeking membership with myself, however hard it is to keep up with all the ways I displace my own image before my situationstory, however doable fingerprinting sounds to the lawmaker matching on my behalf the excess of my *genea*. The affective carnival of existing in body-full shapes, of being from here and from there, of hosting multiple personalities, of disordering time, and of going incognito is the rhizome of a polity from the cartographies of ducks, moths, and vibriyo, (and) not to forget a modernity that has gone autistic (unaware) for lack of metrics. The situation beyond all beyonds where the ordering comes from all algorithms, gives me a biocitizenry in all darkness, in all hysteria. It makes of the abstract a solution of the whole, the way I rotate now. Shall we utter some words?

III.

It started in the year 2010, and the times before that. Before that I held Rue Odeïde. Before 20 Rue Odeïde was another sequence in the normalcy of another genome line permeable to gold, sugarcane, and *terra firma*. The story before all that wasn't the tragedy of girls and boys clogging their hearts with America's broad stripes folded like a baseball balloon, evenly, closely, tightly choked in. Charles Deslondes (then) could freely knit the ground along the Mississippi River, beyond the dawn's early light with a thousand negro feet bursting the air. Today though, the children of the revolution have grown old and decayed, all of them, now, WANTED for reward. Just as lucrative, the Homeland runs itself on biometricizing a good portion of the peoples' feet, a loop going round and around; some to spread across as voracious customers, others mobilized as incapacitated no matter their desire to wave flags, and many more on their knees to dying poor and alien. The Youwès administration hunts for evidence of crimes committed by Haitians. KOMOKODA campaigns *bare anwo bare anba* that *govènman* belongs in jail. *Bèut, la raison du plus fort est toujours la meilleure,* Youwèssiyayès performs a *revolutionoctomy*, and Haitians to produce biometrics under deferred enforced departure; their body parts expire December 4, 2022.

There is something to confess: I have been unwrapping myself very much lately, literally. Lots of things to unravel from: the grains of childhood, a future to pull down, the remains of a city no one ever heard of, the branches of an Osage orange tree, a name buried underground, and the rational assemblage of pre-figured desires that hold me unaware, lethargic, and zealous. (And the manner) I shall go after my studded selves cast away, lured, hidden, discarded, underdeveloped, to pick myself up, in discretion, one stud after another. It is, of course, that inhabiting one's membership is much like a return, a-pick-up-yourself-left-behind in this and in that and in here and in there; a letting oneself catch up with an history era in everywhere elsewhere; a pulling up together ubiquitous *genea* lines from the flow of time, from the stains a place leaves, and from nature's hiccups, just so to witness myself naturally brought together in my excess, in my remains, in my beyonds, *naturellement*. If the dweller follows the trails of her pheromones and sees her selves in the kinships of deer, mammals, and Japanese gardens, who is to say they can't go here or there, they can't be this or that? The lawmaker doesn't see what I see. I see Milan, Congo-Brazzaville, and Cumbia. I see light, bodies in reassemblage. I shall return to Saint-Michel from the pull of whispers, winds, and bowls of rice cooked in lards and *pwa congo sèch*, all of them homes and borders with which I make alive again.

IV.

(The metrics of a Napoleonic) Big Sam says he's one of us, we are kin, we are friends, we don't keep our distance. Youwès flag is raised in the Heartland, Big Sam arrives for flag-raising ceremonies full of mischief like slaveholder Little François who demands twenty-one billion for freedom. Big Sam gets from the children forty percent of the Heartland's GDP to build Youwès economy, with the *kochon Kreyòl* and the *poul mannin* as the ultimate sacrifice. We're okay, except that the children leave the Heartland behind. They shall go work for the Homeland to land in detention centers. And it has become necessary for the water and the land to give themselves a name just so they say, we have a consciousness of being water and *genea* and borderland; just so Little François and Big Sam legitimately inherit the Heartland now. 10,000 bodies fall on the shore of Rivyè Meyè: Sir Youwèn is right, there is always something *wrong wrong wrong* with the children who've always been *poor poor poor*. Izabela begat Descartes; and Descartes begat Clark; and Clark begat Bil. Bil apologizes for drying up the land. Bil gets a pass. Big children, only the big ones, harvest green beans, pineapples, prosperity. At least, the children of the revolution no longer have their necks glued to their own image, or so they think. Continuing their comet-like elliptical diffusion, Big Sam and Little François blow quietly a little further south, next Sudan, next San Salvador, next Liberia, next Honduras, next Nepal, and *next next next* here and everywhere some big little children will make the case they carry Big Sam's *genea*. Every-bud is for selling.

The point being that the Homeland surveying you at a distance has promised to match *genea* and storylines and *genea* and storylines all the while you dwell in shorelines, in doorways, in the slit of the night, in the day's interstices. And your occurring and your naturalness and lines cannot be matched, so your storylines remain unsolvable, irrecuperable, another quake, another blow. In the day that leaves itself behind with no optics of shadow, the first quake, the one which happens without your knowing and calls forth all the others, knows no distance, no *diyène,* no home, no border. There's nothing wrong with you running every direction. July 2016, I saw Marjorie in Paris. Lately, I have been thinking about going to the Saint-Michel Rue Guerrier barrack. I live in the Youwèsey now. I am a grownup now. An electronic bracelet I shall need to rotate from one home to another. I'm not that kid who sees herself naturally in no borders no walls, not anymore, not anymore. Is Assata Shakur making the best of the Homeland in *La Bayamesa*?

Youwèn says it's the children's fault. They say we're the end, we're the beginning of us. We're not the end, we're not the beginning of us, naturally we know better. Sister Ilari doesn't mistake us for the Indians. The fellow standing next to her is missionary worker Brother Joe in search of salvation; and *next-next-next* to Brother Joe is white woman Dolesal who sees in her mirror, a *very-very-very-very* light-skinned black woman with doubly double consciousness. Then, you move away from the close-up view of your orbit to see yourself across homes and rivers running into each other, and the non-end of your barrack in the middle of Ilari's, next to Joe's and Dolesal's together caught in white disease. There's an *òs* that goes unfinished, a future prefacing the past, whiteness whose white runs off, and the dead hanging on the living. You need no (bio) (me) tricks, only to see to sense yourself. Shall I confess, I might be finally at ease with my uneasiness with the *blancs* landholding my Motherland as I am now on Fatherlands prokaryoting; I mean, taking revenge. Of course, being in excess doesn't justify landholding native lands. To nature is to root. A good case for spacetime genomic holes beyond analogical securities is already inscribed beyond lines of correspondence.

V.

There is another way to ground nature, to pull down, literally, across worlds, across history, all things hysteria, all things disavowal, all things excess: you render it responsible with no demands of a distinct outline. The beast found some body; called the children; asked what to do; millions of bones stood up, gathered in council. In that aesthesis, a *genea* can't hold itself for much longer, but is composed and decomposed and re-routed against the *eigentlichkeit* which moves the assembly-line of some human samples. Something more to give, always: sweetgrass border-crossing world geographies, passports, languages, amphibians, and gold seekers. And the children gave away the *kochon kreyòl* no one remembers anymore; their droplets of moistures disassembling family lineages and spilling out (im)possible shrubs no one sees. My own enchantment grew out of my defeated desire for the Homeland, her breast, her line of descent, her lovers, and doubting all of it. There are walls that expose themselves blank, pictures missing from blanketed walls, unseen lines, frontals, and genes on refrigerators doors. I will need a viral circus show for the love of the food I did not grow up with, the breasted language I gave away, the unpaid bread I pleasure with, and all the times I catch myself unaware, unaware, earthquake-like. And there are face lines that can't be snapped; tweets, chirps, and silences unlanguaged; genomes, rhizomes, unnerving absences more daring than walls pictured, and pictured worlds that keep me footed, out-of-line, unhomely, off.

Kevin Carollo lives in Fargo, ND, and is a professor of world literature and writing at Minnesota State University Moorhead. He is author of a chapbook of poems about early onset dementia, *Elizabeth Gregory* (Rain Taxi/OHM Editions), as well as the hybrid non-fiction work *Shred: Running and Being in the End Times* (forthcoming from NDSU Press).

The Ambivalent Homeland of My Name

I am made of the stories I've told, the slow walk of a name, men and women I've never met. I am made of something in their faces or in their hands. Little mannerisms, fleeting thoughts. What survives in the creases of time.
—Giorgio van Straaten, *Il mio nome a memoria*

We are a sad people . . . Always hoping for something else, something better, and always desperate to have it . . . Always uncomfortable. Always beaten down . . . And always with the temptation in our bodies to take our own lives.
—Elio Vittorini, *Conversazione in Sicilia*

Abstract Furies

In the body of the memory of the history of the father of my people,
I am both son and unholy ghost. With the fury of a prodigal angel
in the cancer invading the body of the son of the son of my ancestors.
Reader–deity, take the last train to the heart of the city in the cancer

of my father and the suicide of my people. Reader–deity, make of your
body and your memory the most furious of abstractions. In the name
of the cancer in the body of the father, of the memory of the homeland,
we beseech thee. With a desperate passion akin to the yearning of salmon

in the heart of the suicide of my people. Reader–deity, build a temple
out of your most disparate temptations. To kill the homeland of the body
of the cancer of my father, you must kill the memory of my people. To
gentrify the prison cells of memory so as to make of my body a luxury suite

of history. Reader-deity, tell me what it means to be a suicidal disciple of life everlasting. With the utmost tremulousness and furiousness and desperation. As the dying rabbit sniffing proffered water in the heart of the memory of my front yard. As the cancer of the stepfather, step-

mother, grandmother, grandfather, and so on before him. In the middle of forever I found myself in a dark mood. It was the cancer of memory coursing through the unbearable legacy of the bloodline of my body. Reader-deity, unself me as you would unself yourself. And so unto you,

with the unbearable blood of my people coursing through the body of the memory of my father I hereby relinquish my rites of birth. Reader-deity, read unto and into and through me as you might your own son or daughter or father or mother. Kill the homeland save the man.

My father, Jack Ronald Carollo (March 26, 1942–June 8, 2018), once told me a story about cleaning out his father Tony Carollo's RV in Arizona in the '80s, in which he's going through some of the deceased's papers and comes across two different birth certificates. On one of them, Dad reads his name with a birthplace of Chicago, where he grew up and spent most of his life. Then he claims he saw another birth certificate, just like the first one, except with his birthplace listed as New York City. He wonders which piece of paper tells the true story of his birth.

This story—which itself may or may not be true, which can never be retraced or confirmed on ancestry or genealogy websites, or otherwise verified by some distant family relation, and which ultimately only adds to the lore of a man I grew up mostly estranged from—a full-blooded Sicilian-American who never saw the homeland—is the beginning of a *Godfather*-like trilogy my dad always wanted to write, but never got around to writing. True or not, I have to admit this story had me hooked.

Twelve years ago, in May 2009, I got up one morning in New York City, went to Battery Park, and took the ferry to Ellis Island. I saw images of the various anti-immigrant posters of the day, some in Italian. I went into the computer library, which offered databases of boat manifests and lists of names from a century ago. As I remember, I typed in "Carollo, 1915," and some 200-plus variations of my name came up—all beginning with *C*, all of them taking different and unpredictable journeys to spell out the manifest destiny of Carollo in America.

My father tells me that once upon a time in the American Southwest, some gangsters—I doubt he used the word *mafiosos*—shot up their home in a case of mistaken identity. I don't remember if Dad was home at the time of the drive-by, but I can picture the obligatory black car, the olive-skinned out-of-town city slickers in pinstripe suits in one-hundred-degree weather, cigarettes dangling from their immigrant grimaces—and some sort of modest ranch home in some ruefully named hamlet like Apache Junction riddled with bullets.

They'd gotten the wrong Tony Carollo—or had they? This story would make it into the novel, at any rate; indeed, it would serve as a narrative device to hint at a possible explanation—or a red herring—for the discrepancy in birthplaces that begins the trilogy of my dad's so-called Sicilian-American gangster life.

My mom told me a few years back that her mother, a full-blooded Irishwoman, had Dad's name down as Giacomo Ronaldo Carollo on their wedding program—much to the perplexity of my dad and the people who named him, I assume.

In the '90s, after I'd started studying Italian at college and decided I wanted to be a writer of some sort, Grandma—we never called her *nonna*—told me that I'd get published if I dropped the *o* from my name. I, however, was wholly uninterested in adopting some milquetoast, toffee-nosed, more proper-British-than-thou name like Kevin Carroll.

I remember cajoling her by saying, "But Grandma, ethnic identity, being Italian—it's cool now." Grandma replied, "Drop the *o*."

I was named Kevin to reflect my Irish heritage, and my middle name is Anthony—not Antonio—after my Grandpa—not *nonno*. Long before I came along, the *o*s had been dropping like flies.

Eventually, my younger brother would change her name legally to Buddy Valentine, and I would by default become the last Carollo to carry the family name. It won't be passed on.

American Mirror

Your ancestors were poor invaders
from shithole countries. The mothers
and fathers of your mothers and fathers
suffered from preemptive PTSD, which

they passed on to you. You are so lucky
to be alive and yet so much of you is dead
to the world. Your cellphone is an IED.
You keep a scorecard for joy and never
check all of the above. You know fuck-all
about love. You vote for the lesser of two
Evel Knievels in the mid-term elections.
Every morning is the blessing of a drone
strike missing its target. You are embedded
shrapnel in the collateral damage of each
peacekeeping mission. Your heart is a pie
chart. You have been tasked to guard
against the rapists at the border of your
mirror. You desire velocity in your travel
or some zoom in your cake but you have
nowhere to run. You used to love to say
for fun and cray, even Fahrvernügen.
You crave hive mind on the corpses
of a gazillion bees. You sell your life
to the highest bidder. You say things
are looking up while looking away.
You fire umpteen rounds into today.

I went to high school in Libertyville, Illinois, in the '80s.
This wasn't exactly the land of the *Godfather*, although
Marlon Brando, teenage upstart, did attend LHS before becoming Marlon Brando, famous actor. He didn't
graduate, but legend has it that he got into trouble rid-
ing his motorcycle onto the front steps of the school.

Instead, I came of age in the land of *Ordinary People* and *The Breakfast Club*, and had a locker next to a girl named Annette Carollo. I don't remember talking to her about our name, or about anything much at all—after all, she was a girl, and I was incredibly shy. I feel like my dad mentioned at some point that there was "another Carollo" family line in Chicago, as if that explained anything. I might even be making that line up.

It is Fall Semester 1990, at the University of Wisconsin-Madison. Third-semester Italian is too rudimentary for me, too much of a basic review of the previous year, so I jump a couple semesters in week two and transfer into an Italian conversation and composition course. The course turns out to be taught by a Sicilian named Giuseppe Candela, who is poring over his roster when I introduce myself. Without looking up, he asks me my name.

When I get to "Carollo," he stops writing and looks at me for the first time. He grins widely, then vigorously shakes my hand. "There is a Carollo in Carini who makes pizza, and he is a magician," Giuseppe says. For the first time, I hear a homeland in the echo of my name. I must find out where Carini is and start planning my prodigal return, one pizza at a time.

I write to Grandma about learning Italian and wanting to know more about where we come from. She never writes back. She never mentions anything about Sicily or Italy or family history, not even when I finish grad school and move close to her in Arizona briefly in August of 2000. I tell her about reading a novel in Italian titled *La gallina volante*—the flying hen—and she laughs enigmatically.

In 1991, after graduating from UW, I take a road trip across the country with my friend David Hamburger, whose parents live in Tarzana, California. Stopping to gas up at some random town in Nevada one morning, I see a kind of supper club in an empty parking lot across the way: *CAROLLO's*. I think, *What are the odds?*

In the mid-'80s, not long before Tony Carollo passes, he discovers I've never eaten his wife's eggplant parmesan. "You've never had your grandma's eggplant parmesan?" he asks incredulously. "You're not half-dago!"

Nancy Carollo would outlive her husband Tony by a quarter century, and I consider myself fortunate to have enjoyed her eggplant parmesan one night in Mesa, Arizona, in late 2000 when she was eighty-six years old— shortly before moving back to Illinois to live with Dad and Wilma, shortly before stopping cooking altogether.

American Childhood

I never outkicked anyone,
except for this one time
during the eighth-grade half

at the high school track,
when in the final stretch,
I took the lead and crossed

the line like Prefontaine—
I believe I clocked a 2:29—
and thought I could see

my grandpa cheering me
on from the stands, exactly
the way he might root

for the horses he bet on,
a desperate Sicilian who
can hardly believe he's won,

and who afterwards gushed
in proud disbelief that I'd
destroyed my unsuspecting

peers, as if with this measly
victory all of the diaspora
might yet be saved. Anyone,

especially me, was down for
such a yarn. I was a kid
who'd do just about anything

to save some face or please
someone else. I didn't realize
until several lifetimes later

that in running, as in life,
you are mostly competing
against yourself. And though

Grandpa never attended
another meet, and though
I never outkicked anyone ever

again, I made sure to keep
my desultory pursuers at bay.
I always made sure I made

enough of a statement at
the outset that the thought
of reeling me in was to meet

the ancient ire of his stare,
watching his "half-dago" grandson,
who broke the tape and won.

In 2006, I'm finally going to Sicily for the first time, the
only known Carollo in the family to visit the homeland

since an aunt I've never met allegedly made the pilgrimage in the early '70s. I'd asked my dad if he could scare up any info on the family homeland, and he ends up leaving a signature rambling message on my old-school answering machine, the basic gist of which is: you have to go through the Maggiores or Gravagnas—family names I've never heard before—to figure out the history of the Carollos. *You can't trust the Carollos*, my dad warns, *because they lived with the animals.*

At the time, I just thought my dad was crazy. Later on, I would read about how class hierarchies often played out in Sicily, with the landed gentry keeping historical records while the human beasts of burden lived with their animal brethren, working the land and maintaining the estates of their masters. Hidden in my dad's incoherent message lay a profound revelation about what drove the myriad Sicilian migrations to the industrialized north of Italy and the Americas.

Dad also mentions the name of a town, which he doesn't spell, but which I look up and figure out is basically a suburb east of Palermo: Bagheria, which Peter Robb in *Midnight in Sicily* describes as a Mafia enclave in the '70s. I recall reading about one summer month in particular where upwards of some seventy gang-related murders occurred on the streets of Bagheria, but today I can't find the exact passage.

I've booked a flat for two weeks in a building not quite up to code in the heart of Palermo, right next to the Bellarù market. It is the late fall of 2009. I have nothing to do and no one to talk to most days, which I spend walking around Palermo with no destination in mind. I drink cheap wine and write lousy lonely poems in the flat while local revelers party late into the night.

One afternoon, I enter a random bookstore to browse absentmindedly for a few minutes. Completely by chance, I come across a collection of three plays entitled *Carnezzeria*, which turns out to be a *trilogia della famiglia siciliana* ("trilogy of the Sicilian family") by Palermo-born playwright Emma Dante. The first play, *mPalermu* (*In Palermo*), is written in Sicilian dialect and concerns one Sunday morning in the life of *la famiglia* CAROLLO.

I don't know how long I look at the cast of five Carollos on page 21 of the collection, how long it takes to register that Dante has chosen my name—with the same exact spelling—to signify a typical Sicilian family. The play itself is absurdist in nature, about the poor Carollo "everyfamily" simply trying to leave the house for a dignified Sunday walk in their Sunday best, and failing to do so.

It would perhaps be an act of questionable vanity on my part to translate this tragicomic story of the Carollo family, but in some deep-seated way I feel called by name to do so. According to Emma Dante, the play *Carnezzeria*—which might be roughly translated as "bloodbath" or "slaughter"—concerns "people torn from themselves, slaughtered (*scannati*) by a dull and insignificant (*insulsa*) life. Frightened and dangerous animals who, because of their profound capacity to participate in the suffering of others, in time end up losing every connection with their humanity (*ogni parentela umana*)."

This is also a rough translation.

Three years before Palermo, and shortly after my first trip to the homeland, I see Annette Carollo at our twenty-year high-school reunion in Libertyville, Illinois. She's working in the Virgin Islands, which sounds interesting enough, but what I really want to talk about is the slow walk, or *lento cammino*, of the Carollo name. As soon as I say "Sicily," however, Annette interrupts to inform me that all her relatives come from Northern Italy, not Sicily. I think to myself, *Yeah, that's just what they told you.*

He called me honey ... *called me honey*

He had Wilma call from her cell.

The cancer had spread to his lungs.

They had moved to Marengo of all

I got the feeling he'd be refusing

places. He wished he had better news.

the chemo. Back in Huntley, Wilma

He called me honey. He said he had

was trying to clean some things up.

a favor to ask of me when I got back

I could tell she was very worried

from Italy. A favor regarding Wilma.

about leaving my dad all alone.

This was just last Wednesday. I told

This is just the latest sad chapter

him that he had nothing to worry

in the story of their life together as

about. I told him I could just as well

told by the American Dream. Dad

cancel my trip and come see him

and I never made it to Italy but we

instead. He said there was no need.

shared a day in Paris once. We also

I asked him if he'd talked to anyone

went to a Vietnam veterans art museum

else, and he said not yet. For some

in Chicago in the '90s. When we happened

dumb reason, I said, "Thank you, Dad,

upon a series of black and white photos

for calling me first." And he said, "Well,

of headless and mangled bodies in

you're my oldest." And then I lost it.

a jungle backdrop called the American

I completely lost it. I told him Wilma

legacy, Dad said, "Saw a lot of that."

had nothing to worry about. The day

I almost lost it. I had to believe him.

after tomorrow I'm supposed to get

I guess I'd like Dad's god to offer some

on a plane and leave this godforsaken

alternative facts to the latest war on his

country for the first time in a good five

mind and body. What kind of eulogy is

years. I can't say at this point I even

"He kept up with what I was up to as

want to go. I can hardly keep up

best he could" or "He called me honey"?

with the latest school shooting or

On a park bench in Paris he told me about

celebrity sexual predator. I can only

the time in Vietnam when, if he'd leaned in

think about the tragic figure of my

closer (like so) to his buddy at the time, it

father who served in Vietnam early

could have been the end for either one of them.

on. Early on in our conversation I

To think I'd taken the better part of

knew something was up. What if

a lifetime to feel the wind of a sniper's

every memory is a sniper in waiting?

bullet lodged inside my father's heart.

What if our legacy is to remain

> *To think I might only and forever be*
utter mysteries unto one another?
> *the lone gunman of my father's memory.*

I was in Sicily when my father died, which turned out to be the day Anthony Bourdain took his own life in the south of France. Anthony, like Grandpa Carollo, like my middle name. I'd written the above poem the week before in Naples—at the Hotel Gramsci, as it happens—while wondering what the fuck I was doing in Italy when Dad was dying back home in Illinois. I spoke to him for the last time during the layover in O'Hare, not even cognizant of the now-obvious fact that he was dying a mere half hour or so west of the airport I was currently in. I like to think that we both thought we would have more time, but of course we never do.

The day Dad was dying, I went with a friend to an open-air performance of Euripides's *Hercules* at the Teatro Greco in Siracusa. The Greek tragedy opens with a dying father waiting in vain for the return of his prodigal son. With the exception of some members of the chorus, the cast was entirely female, and directed by none other than one Emma Dante.

I like to think the watch I bought the next day to honor Dad—my dad who loved watches—offers a recursive and circular view of time to prodigal son and father alike. I like to think the elusive connection between me, my father, and our ancestral homeland is evoked by the elegant and beautiful memento of Sicily strapped to my left wrist. But I also know it's not true.

My dad—an obsessive and inveterate book collector—loved science fiction, Westerns, and tales of adventure most of all. He loved reading about adventurers going where no one had ventured before, an intrepid cast of characters striking out Bourdain-style to parts unknown—the very antithesis of the Carollo family depicted in Emma Dante's play. In such stories, people rarely return to their home planet, and when they do, it's almost always scarcely recognizable. Most of the time, in fact, home is nowhere to be found.

I like to think that Dad is okay with that.

Michelle Matthees lives in Duluth, Minnesota, where she works in the public schools and as an Uber driver. She's recently been awarded grants from the Minnesota State Arts Board and The Arrowhead Regional Arts Council. Her first book-length collection of poems *Flucht* was published by New Rivers Press.

Lite Brite

For one month all you wanted

was a Lite Brite, a mixing of
diffusion and explosion of light

fingertip ready. The glass pegs—

that one hovering between orange
and pink—had tiny bubbles within,

an astronaut's secret air supply

only seen once lit. The whole house
dark. It was so satisfactory, poking

pegs through black paper sheet,
the white Y for yellow,

B for blue. Those were

the cleanest brush stokes ever.
You could tell

the truth about the Lite Brite,

its demise, your attempts
at its salvation via electrician's tape

while eating burnt peanut butter toast

but since you've committed
yourself to survival, instead, you'll speak

about the warmth, being

saved by mass production and Da Vinci,
whose light couldn't help but escape

from everything.

The Bargain

When you are in your father's arms
falling down the stairs,

and those stairs rise to meet you

like the slipperiest accordion
crumpling inward off-tune,

and the bargain has been made

to survive these next seconds—
the tree rips through

the second story biblically, sending

a squirrel loose above into the rooms
of your house, a newly minted

Darwinian maze. *Save me, oh*

again, divvy up the day
because your mother tells the same story

and how you three sang *You*

are my sunshine against
the framed torque and flooded

basement. You have no memory

of that, the song,
but you like its idea,

a lightbulb when the electricity's

cut. Must you trust her
happiness? Yes, or you

won't make it.

Babushka in the Basement

Tan tile, misshapen and broken,
this is where the men go

with shotguns and stolen hoses,

bags of rock salt bigger
than you, and a vice

mounted tight to railroad ties,

a pedestrian starscape
of peg board with tools

hanging in coarse constellations.

Someone else is in the basement.
She summons you

from the melted beer bottle

ashtray with a woman on it
outlined in white.

She shades you

with broken garden wings.
She is one thing

you won't lift from the basement

where she suckled
unclaimed pain

showing what you shouldn't have

known: life
at the very core of a dense tree,

schist that sparkles but never sees

the sun, the precise weight of a
dead snow goose, white

in your childhood arms.

She claimed you and let you go, laughing
and watching you head for the sun.

You promise to write and you don't.

Artress Bethany White is a poet, essayist, and literary critic living in New Jersey. She is the recipient of the Trio Award for her poetry collection *My Afmeria* (Trio House Press, 2019) and author of *Survivor's Guilt: Essays on Race and American Identity* (New Rivers Press, 2020). Her prose and poetry have appeared in such journals as *Harvard Review, POETRY, Solstice, Birmingham Poetry Review, Tupelo Quarterly, The Hopkins Review, Green Mountains Review*, and the forthcoming anthology *Why I Wrote This Poem: 62 Poets on Creating Their Works* (McFarland, 2022). She is associate professor of English at East Stroudsburg University, teaches poetry and nonfiction workshops for the Rosemont College Summer Writer's Retreat in Pennsylvania, and is nonfiction editor for Boston-based *Pangyrus* literary magazine. Check out her website at artressbethanywhite.com.

How to Write a Protest Poem Amid a Pandemic

Resistance is possible. Resistance is not only possible, but it is the only legitimate response to these systems and apparatuses of unfreedoms.
—Angela Y. Davis, speaking at Southern Illinois University Carbondale, February 13, 2014

In June 2020, I found myself teaching a weeklong writing workshop on crafting memoir in times of crisis. The theme was reflective of a unique moment in the United States: a coalescing of Black Lives Matter protests, the COVID-19 pandemic, and the ever-looming threat of climate crisis. One afternoon during our video class meeting, a participant declared with candid frustration, "I wish I could just be out there protesting right along with them." Quite aware of the many reasons why she could not, I suggested to her that she was protesting, but instead of the streets, she was using the page.

To resist is to participate in the art of resurrection; this is literary activism. It is writing that springs from the realization that a system has failed and a new construction must be engineered from its ruins.

I was ushered into the practice of literary activism by scholar activist Angela Y. Davis. I recall purchasing a copy of the 1974 book *Angela Davis: An Autobiography* from a sidewalk bookseller on the Lower East Side of New York in the nineties. The cover featured a photograph of her signature no-nonsense Afro—follicular resistance at its finest. Around this time, I came across fliers and other ephemera related to the Black Panthers at a used bookstore in the same neighborhood, pages I read through, but never purchased. I eagerly digested these stories of protest and resistance, and became familiar with the intimate bond between intellectualism and social change. Before long, my voracious reading segued into pursuit of a graduate degree at New York University, where I attended lectures by scholars like Paul Gilroy, Hazel Carby, and Isaac Julien. In this arena, I came to understand that my racial burden as a Black woman was not my true inheritance but a misplaced social construct created for me as a byproduct of being born Black in America. I saw a pattern emerging: American democracy was for the few, and a life of resistance for the many. Message received, I began to write.

When COVID-19 hit, some U.S. residents were encouraged by their state governors to don face masks against its spread, and almost immediately I began to see social-media posts from Black men being profiled as criminals while masking. At first, when nonmedical masks were not widely available as infection rates began to escalate, many resorted to wearing Western-style bandanas tied around their faces as protection. Under less sobering circumstances, it might have been laughable to see so many folk suddenly strutting around like cartoon bandits. For Black men, however, the makeshift mask became just another liability during desperate times. This was not new news; the biased mistreatment of Black people is often the de facto measure of social anxiety amid times of crisis, and the nation would soon erupt in ways that many of us had only previously imagined. National history has taught us there must always be a sacrificial lamb culled from the disenfranchised to sustain American freedom. We in the Black literary community have adopted the practice of naming the lambs over and over again; first, recently deceased Black men, women, and children populate our hearts; then, ultimately, our verse.

The natural world, however, did not require such diabolic sacrifice. For my family and me, the apparent normalcy outside our Philadelphia lockdown doors bespoke a hopeful future for us all. From late March through June, spring bloomed within the plant and animal kingdom the same as always: ubiquitous azaleas and roses burst forth in determined shades of purple, pink, and white, while newborn groundhogs scurried after lumbering adults. The fecundity of new life was encouraging, but as I watched I knew even this unburdened display was, in some ways, fallacious.

Though the world watched with awe the proof of air-borne pollution abating in places from Los Angeles to Mumbai, we somehow knew one woe could not be easily traded out for another. I had already seen sporadic reports of animals of various species being carriers of coronavirus. Yet the tone of these species-oriented rumblings was low, and not one of those infected tigers, housecats, or mink could be spotted striving toward wellness as easily as the masked human.

When I first spied a robin fly away from a meticulously constructed nest within this swirl of springtime grandeur, I knew her treasure must be contained inside. Surreptitiously, I crept closer and peered over the nest's edge. Sure enough, three turquoise eggs lay within a layered web of straw and twigs. In turn, the nest neatly hugged the solid, white brick wall just under the rear-yard eaves of our two-story colonial. I understood immediately that this robin and I were caught in primal relationship; two houses backing each other up, full of offspring—avian alongside human—being nurtured for survival.

Our family walked our neighborhood every day during lockdown. Survival dictated this time of exercise and meditation. Each step measured out minutes of virus-free life, and they were precious. We did not walk alone. On the sidewalks, nearby neighbors mirrored our behavior. There were so few cars on the road that lanes of people used the streets too, reminding us of episodes of *The Walking Dead*. We shambled, not unlike zombies, stunned by the rules of our new existence.

My family and I watched over our innocent robin and her crafted domicile, making sure we did not disturb her too many times by entering the backyard after seeing her startle and fly away whenever we stepped near. The nest became our beacon of hope. We knew she needed to sit atop her eggs, warm them into birds whose beaks would one day strike out with enough enthusiasm to bring them into the world.

It was our oldest son, whose bedroom perched one floor above the robin's nest, who complained one morning about raucous bird cries, a strident maternal protest, that awoke him at 5:30 in the morning. Immediately, my husband and I feared the worst: our nest had been attacked by daybreak marauders. When we looked in on the hatchlings, they appeared suddenly too still, yellow beaks resting motionless against the interior curve of the nest walls. We turned away in sorrow, suddenly finding ourselves negligent watchmen. As we departed for a family outing, masks in hand to protect our own lives, every head hung low for the fallen.

When I checked the contents of the nest the next day, I found two beaks pointed skyward and slightly parted, like the lips of tweezers, in a clear aspect of hunger. My peripheral vision caught mother robin hopping industriously toward her nest, mouth bulging with a large burgundy worm. The hatchlings had not died after all; we had merely mistaken slumber for death. I ran into the kitchen to share the good news. One by one, every family member made the pilgrimage outside to prove to themselves that indeed we could lay our mourning aside. Our two families still moved in tandem toward the future.

The U.S. body politic has always been a contested, exclusionary space, full of barriers and hurdles erected to keep out those already marginalized by race, class, gender, sexual orientation, and religious difference. Over time, it has presented itself as a just-out-of-reach heaven on earth, requiring all who seek its protection to separate themselves from their once-nurturing communities in order to gain access to its often still-hostile, privileged center. In spring 2020, as the pandemic raged, two Black men and a Black woman—Ahmaud Arbery, George Floyd, and Breonna Taylor—were murdered within four months of each other. The rarified space of this center became all too clear again; humanity watched as Black Lives Matter protests became proof of life and catalyst for change.

As COVID-19 continued its insidious spread, Asian Americans emerged as another community forced into survival mode by discrimination and violence initiated from the nation's highest political office. All signs pointed to Wuhan, China, as ground zero of the virus; illogically, suddenly people going about their daily lives were singled out for blame, vilified by biased U.S. groupthink. Every Asian person became Chinese in these people's view, regardless of ethnic origin. Newsfeeds filled with sobering photographs of Asian men with purpled cheeks and blackened eyes, and narratives by Asian women explaining in vivid detail being spit upon or verbally harangued on the street for bringing the coronavirus from China. This story did not change much, even as updated information revealed that Europe was the actual site of origin for the spread of the disease along the East Coast.

But racist violence and a raging pandemic were not the only woes the country faced. A week after we celebrated our surviving birds, a derecho hit our Philadelphia neighborhood. Cell phones buzzed throughout the house, alerting everyone to stay indoors and prepare for strong winds. We watched as the sky darkened into a faux dusk and a whipping wind ended our weather gazing on the porch. I sprinted inside as my husband struggled to close the front door, the fingers of both hands wrapped around its edge. A fleeting image of one of Dorothy's family members trying to shut the cellar door in *The Wizard of Oz* flashed through my mind.

A mere fifteen minutes later, we'd lost electricity, along with dozens of fully established oak and maple trees. The trees had literally been ripped from the earth and flung onto their sides, roots dangling like tentacles in the air, with concrete sidewalks torn asunder beneath them. I marveled at the level of destruction, so out of proportion to what weather reports had warned us about. Later I would learn that derechos can reach a wind speed mirroring that of a Category 4 hurricane. As I roamed the neighborhood that day, taking pictures of downed trees, police-taped street closures, and cars crushed by these same fallen trees, I considered the reality of human fragility in the face of this new climate monster.

Back at home, rounding the corner of our house, I saw the bird nest still wedged snugly against the wall. I was disappointed when I discovered it was empty.

I worked to calculate time, something that had become difficult to do during the pandemic. After hatching, robins develop in their nests for two weeks before they are strong enough to jump out. I reasoned that the birds could have been old enough to leave the nest with an assist from their mother and perhaps make it to safer, higher ground. But my family speculated that the missing robins had been swept out to pasture by the derecho. Everyone searched for shattered bird bodies in the nearby grass, but found none. Without the evidence, there was possibility. When two of us voiced our optimism and claimed the birds were actually old enough to have survived, the naysayers allowed that bubble of hope to hang suspended before our eyes, drawing us together again.

No, it did not surprise me when Ahmaud Arbery was cornered and killed by a white father and son in Georgia. The elaborately staged murder represented the stark failure of the United States to address its systemic racism for generations. This national neglect has led to generational racism easily passed from father to son and mother to daughter, nurture cleaving stubbornly to doctrine. My response to the murder was to do what poets do: I began to compose a poem. Only after completing it days later did I realize that, within the seven couplets comprising this grimly themed ghazal, I had situated Ahmaud Arbery in a historical continuum of African Americans—Frederick Douglass, Harriet Jacobs, the children of Sally Hemings—all of whom had once been enslaved and escaped their bondage. Arbery, born a free man, was the only one who had run and died trying. How to write a protest poem amid a pandemic? Do not suppress the rise of historical, ethical, and political dismay.

I could not include the name of every Black life lost due to social and institutional injustice in a single poem. In the time I penned and began to revise my poem toward completion, at least three new lives were taken; three more families left shaken to their core. The tearing away of a family member involves the mingling of tears and shameless snot. The pounding of breasts. The pressing of temples between clenched fists, and the hoarse, ragged call on the divine. The ritual a cadence befitting the open wound following an untimely death.

Today, if I were to look for any hope of a human resurrection amid protest as resistance, it would lie in this truth: the United States once freed the enslaved of this nation, and the constitutional language of that feat remains. This simple fact proves that my country is more than capable of freeing the post-emancipation descendants re-enslaved by educational, employment, and health inequity. If there is any hope in a poem written about the intellectual chattel who once ran to embrace freedom, and the video of a twenty-first century Black man who died trying in Georgia, it is this unequivocal truth. In times of pandemic, irresponsible leadership, and police violence, I choose to meditate on injustice in as many subtle and stark iterations as possible, through metered and free verse and prose. For me, that's the nature of poetry in a time of protest and disease: a series of resurrections born of resistance.

Mandy-Suzanne Wong's latest book is the PEN/Galbraith-nominated essay collection *Listen, we all bleed.*, published by New Rivers Press in 2021. Her novel *Drafts of a Suicide Note*, published by Regal House, was a Foreword INDIES finalist and PEN Open Book Award nominee; and her short story duet *Awabi* won the Digging Press Chapbook Series Award. *The Box*, her next novel, is forthcoming from Graywolf Press. She lives in Bermuda.

A Foot on the Sky

He emerges from a packet of his brothers in his own good time. He is in motion from the first of his blue moments. He does a bit of sinking: his first sensation is of the possessiveness of home. But his first thought is of that very water buoying him up should he so choose, and so he does. Because he feels he can, he unfurls the sails to either side of his tiny face. And he is swimming for the first time, spinning spirals none too steady. Blue is his first vision, blue all around him, everywhere, caressing his microscopic tentacles. Blue flooding him with love and courage of oceanic potency is instantly the meaning of home.

His brothers teeter off on their curly adventures. His father, if he had one, sailed away long ago. His blue home does all the rocking that his mother doesn't, having no knowledge of or interest in his existence. The ocean sweeps him away from her at the first opportunity, drawing him to its blue sighing heart and

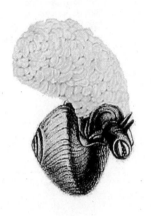

nourishing him of itself, gifting particles to the cilia on his sails. The ocean teaches him to distinguish vibrations, taste with his entire body, question the warm threshold where yellow light lancing from above turns blue.

The ocean is his first and last great love. His one wish is to hold onto it forever. He will listen to its colors and express his love with his whole self. His foot begins to grow, his expression of his one wish: a lifelong attachment.

If he were an abalone, he'd descend to the ocean floor and crawl in search of his ancestors' slime trails, hoping to follow them to the colony. Were he a turban snail, he'd follow his liquid sense of time's uneven oscillations to a memory (not his own) of algae in whose sheltering embrace he could let himself stop swimming. But he isn't that sort of snail. His yearning won't be satisfied by family, food, or anything that stone or seagrass has to offer. He doesn't want a sandy burrow or coral metropolis. He loves the ocean as its liquid self.

He sees rays of yellow light grasp the water from above like giant cilia. He sees the ocean grasp the light and change it into its own blue. He feels the light give itself up to a metamorphosis into the ocean's intrinsic warmth. He makes for the gleaming threshold where the water meets the light. The shell hanging heavy on his neck below his sails, the light, too bright, blaring in his lidless eyes, make him think of giving up and sinking. But love outswims frustration. Though his stubby shell can't be made to pull him up instead of down, he cannot let it go, he has plans for it. Up he swims, his face burning; his gooey outstretched foot is all he has for grasping. It requires turning upside down, up-thrusting his foot into the burning, where he grasps the edge, presses his body to the sharp edge where the light clutches the ocean and the ocean transfigures the light.

He'll spend his life there, bound to the open ocean; clinging by its underside to the surface, surfing on the sunlit sky with his one foot. He'll devote himself to sculpting his devotion, nurturing his attachment, and with everything he has, not least his pelagic sense of history, paying tender tribute to his great love.

He is far from alone. The neustonic community, whose home is the waving, raining, vaporizing border between sea and air, includes hydrozoans, planktonic anemones, jellyfishes, baby fishes and octopuses, blue nudibranchs, tiny crustaceans. In meadows of Sargassum weed, brown-spotted frogfishes hang by toes and elbows from the algae's bristly fronds, which sprout golden bubbles like hollow berries to stay afloat. The plastic undead haunt the neuston day and night. Squatters brave and desperate overrun soda bottles and unwanted shoes. Many are poisoned or suffocated by pollutants. No one who lives there can do anything about them.

It's a place between worlds, the neuston. As a threshold it is neither here nor there. It's ambiguous and contentious. And for this little holoplanktonic snail, it's home. It's a home that has nothing whatsoever to do with security, belonging, or resources. The only assurance he needs is that his attachment to his love will be unbreakable. He has nothing but resolve and his soft little body with which to achieve it.

Upside down at the surface, he imagines that his foot is like the cilia of light. With the back end of his sole, his small propodium, he probes the light. Its aridity and harsh texture astonish him, but he'll grow used to them in time. He forms a scoop with his propodium to catch a bit of air and light. Just a bit of air and light—as if with cupped hands, he catches it. He scoops it and kneads it into his very own bubble. He wraps his bubble in blue-violet mucus summoned from deep down inside him. In blue-violet, like a painter, he sings his wish to grasp the ocean like the light, his longing to be held and be made blue. He catches another bubble, joyful, another and another. His enthusiasm stitches them together violet-blue. So delighted is he with them that he decides to keep them all. He holds onto all his bubbles with his foot.

From that moment, he lives on a raft of bubbles attached to the ocean's surface by its underside—and by a love so strong that his bubbles endure downpours, cyclones, and the ocean's moods with almost polyacrylate steadfastness. He devotes himself, body and mind, to caring for his raft; he makes repairs and renovations. For what is this structure of mucus-coated air but the embodiment, expression, and site of this tiny being's affection for another vast and deep. The bubble raft is home and life itself to him. He knows that if he let his bubbles go, the shell on his back, hanging down under the water, would drag him into the abyss. There he would die of starvation and despair, for he can no longer swim.

That shell, a self-made spiral of aragonite and calcite, is what makes him a mollusk. The shell in its own way is his mobile home. And yet aside from hungry turtles, this very shell, a stiff and heavy burden, poses the greatest danger to his life in the neuston. His risk of sinking grows in proportion to that shell. His dependence on his raft grows in like proportions as he secretes his own peril and bears it on his back.

Other pelagic snails, the gymnosomes, cast off their shells when they reach adulthood. But for him such an act would be unthinkable. For him, no gymnosome but *Janthina janthina*, his shell is his masterpiece; it is his unique creation, a masterwork of sculpture and color, his absolutely personal expression of undying love. Inspired by oceanic curls and ripples, he secretes a spiral of his own, just one. He adds to it each day, and from the fluids of his body he makes colors. Where shell and bubbles meet, he dyes the former dark blue-violet, seeming from above to meld with the adumbral deep. The shell's underside he paints lavender-blue, so from below he blends in with the sunlit sky-kissed sea. With his body he memorializes his home threshold between worlds. He dedicates his creation to the ocean.

His artistry confounds aliens like ourselves. How does a small, slimy invertebrate learn to make complicated and expressive things? The quickest way to make ourselves feel better about this is to dismiss the water-breather's creation of a raft of air as "instinctive," thus mechanical and thoughtless. An expedient hypothesis: his inconvenient shell of its inimitable blue (a sacred blue in the Torah, at whose command have perished millions of snails) is an automatic product or byproduct of Evolution, that progressive manufacturer of living things.

He'd say something quite different if anyone knew how to ask him. Experience has taught him that time moves at different speeds concurrently. Oceanic currents ripple and wave at multiple speeds in several directions simultaneously in every moment, causing moments to vary unpredictably in size, which enables a seasnail to remember what he'd never known. Extra-aquatic aliens have no hope of understanding this. But to him it is simple, it makes perfect sense: that memories originating with the dead and fossilized should be his memories too. How far back in time he remembers, precisely which historic trails he follows with his porous mind, we extra-aquatics cannot conceive.

We can only wonder: Who were these deft ancestors of his? Snails who crawled along the ocean floor wouldn't have made bubbles, for they couldn't reach the sky. The ancient nautilids, big-brained, free-swimming, few of whom remain today, did make shells with chambers around their outer edges, which the animals filled with gas in precise measures to maintain their buoyancy. Perhaps it's only that the nautilus keeps his bubbles inside his shell, keeps his creations for himself instead of making colorful offerings; in which case the janthinid would say it's he himself who loves his ocean best. He has given up swimming in order to devote himself to architectural oblations. He has no effort to spare for self-propulsion. He lacks the means to make it easier, like foot extensions or a siphon. Whiffs of breeze, the smallest ripples, sweep him dizzily here and there. And it's a matter of pride with him, entrusting his fate to the ocean.

With his face turned ever sunward, his eyes deteriorate. He's barely an adult when blindness overtakes him. It is terrifying, the withdrawal of the blue like the world falling out from under him. But he still feels the ocean, feels it swaddling and rocking. His first vision is still with him, the ocean blue and the light of the sky. He knows he is not forsaken, he must pull himself together and go on. His love and work take on a desperate quality. His bubble raft grows long and thick, outgrowing its creator, becoming twice his size as he holds on for all he's worth.

Dining is a problem now that he has lost his sight. As soon as he'd decided what his life's work would be, he had consumed the little sails of his larvahood: he ate himself as early nourishment for his great effort. Now a growing adult who spends every moment clinging to the intangible, he must trust entirely to chance and to the ocean. He's inherited a taste for jellyfishy hydrozoans. He likes by-the-wind sailors and Portuguese men o' war, whose deadly stings are nothing to him. They too are neuston drifters following oceanic fancies.

He starts to taste the hydrozoans when the ocean brings them near and they collide. His small cloud of blue-violet paint hypnotizes them into higher states of mind; metaphysical enchantments absorb their entire colonies' collective consciousness. They don't recoil when he squeezes his mouth out of his head between his tentacles, when he erodes them with his teeth-en-crusted tongue. As he eats, she carries on with her creative work. Food may be important, but it is not her priority. Catching bubbles, crafting spirals in vio-let-blue love songs, these are her first concerns. Intent on showering her ocean in gifts of complex forms and colors, she is but partially attentive to meals. When she is hungry and collides with other janthinids, she eats them as distractedly as she does hydrozoans.

We call her "she" now, on account of an inner ritu-al. An obligation which, according to her sense of his-tory, the ocean expects of her. Though her new organs are sometimes uncomfortable, they do not interrupt her work. Nor do they change her way of thinking, nor alter her priorities in the slightest. Should condi-tions in her ocean home require it, she could go back to being him. Chancing to bump into a male or not, possibly accomplishing the whole thing herself with hermaphroditic elegance, she drops some pellets at some point. That each pellet is a packet of thirty twin-sailed brothers she does not care and may not know. With all her being, she is intent on bubbles, blues, and spirals, just as she has been from the first of her blue moments. Driven by a love that is not vanity nor any illusion of her species' immortality, she loves her ocean not as payment for its protection. She knows her bubble collection and thin blue-violet shell, each a few centimeters long, could do nothing for her against turtles, birds, or big fishes. Vulnerability and contingency are as fundamental to her notions of home life as absolute dependency on the vast and roiling stranger she adores.

As for that shell of hers, an alien might go so far as to say that it is useless, irrelevant to the violet snail's survival. We might go further, caring less for janthinids' marvelous being than the conformity of all existence to our conceptions of the world: we might say, given the occurrence of shell-free gymnosomes, that Evolution should have done away with janthinids. "Survival of the Fittest," that straightforward algorithm, should have eliminated snails who, unable to swim or see, are unfit for open-ocean living. Compared to crawling snails, she is equally ridiculous. She does everything upside down. Her obsession with bubbles is inappropriate. On the seafloor she'd be hopeless at finding anything to eat.

Having gone to such extremes in fashioning her home, she has failed to live up to either proper neuston-dwellers or proper snails and failed to die in compliance with Natural Selection.

Since Natural Selection is the predominant scientific model of biological progress, no evolutionary history which has so far been proposed for janthinids succeeds in making sense. No matter how we aliens envision their phylogeny, they appear to have come out of nowhere for no reason, the rightful descendants and precursors of nobody. Notwithstanding evolutionary pressures like pollution and climate collapse, violet snails nevertheless remain abundant.

Believing her existence to have been a mistake, some kind of error in the algorithm's execution, is less of a bother than trying to circumvent or bore a peephole through the predominant scientific model of biological progress. We extra-aquatics delineate the horizons of familiarity and comfort by building just such conceptual models to structure our thinking. Our structures become habitual, our habits the stoutest walls of our habitat, often with bricked-up windows. Snug in the prefabricated comforts of our self-affirming concepts, we aliens may look at *Janthina janthina* and think she's got it all wrong, she has misunderstood everything from the meaning of life and usefulness to snailhood itself, the ocean, and the very idea of home.

For it seems sometimes that everything she does is for nothing; her invulnerable love, her perfect devotion, her work, bubbles and blues in honor of her ocean. She might have sailed to Scotland or through the Strait of Gibraltar to Sardinia and Crete, the wind in her bubbles and thousands of fellow snails borne on Trans-Atlantic storms to turn long stretches of sand as purple as hillsides of blooming heather. Extreme weather events are after all on the increase as the ocean overheats. But when the latest storm subsides, leaving her ocean bilious and absentminded, as if discomposed by an attack of fever, she isn't far at all from where she was born. She is so little and light that a thoughtless shrug from her great blue love casts her tumbling and reeling into an alien realm.

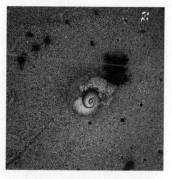

Suddenly she feels what no janthinid should ever feel. She feels beneath her back—solidity. With terrible bouncing and a jolt, she runs aground. The ocean withdraws. The ocean leaves her on the sand. She cannot understand it and she cannot breathe, but she believes the ocean will come back for her. She is lying on her side. She has only to wait. Her great love will return, will take care of her on the next wave . . .

She is waiting. A clump of seaweed lands beside her. She retreats into her shell as far as she can, to the secret gasp of moisture there. Sand speckled pink by foraminifera rasps against her bubbles, but they do not break. She is frightened, her mechanoreceptors are confused, but her raft does not break. She is sliding sideways, she tumbles head over foot and does not break. She is rolling, becoming weightless, tasting salt, salt the joy and relief of water scooping her up, rushing in over her head, washing her bubbles clean of sand. Faster than any other snail has ever flown, she sweeps out to sea on the breath of her ocean, going home. Her bubbles, airy light, seek out the sky. Her raft rights itself, blue-violet, and she sails on.

Images

Janthina janthina. Watercolor by Charles Alexandre Lesueur, *Voyage de découvertes* (Paris: Imprimerie Impériale, 1807), xxxi. Wikimedia Commons, public domain.

Janthina janthina with seaweed (*Sargassum spp.*), Horseshoe Bay, Bermuda, 2021. Photo by Carmelita Tucker. Reproduced by kind permission.

References

Betti, Federico, G. Bavestrello, M. Bo, M. Coppari, F. Enrichetti, M. Manuele, and R. Cattaneo-Vietti. "Exceptional strandings of the purple snail *Janthina pallida* Thompson 1840 (Gastropoda: Epitoniidae) and first record of an alien goose barnacle along the Ligurian coast (western Mediterranean Sea)." *The European Zoological Journal* 84, no. 1 (2017): 488-495. https://doi.org/10.1080/24750263.2017.1379562.

Beu, Alan. "Evolution of *Janthina* and *Recluzia* (Mollusca: Gastropoda: Epitoniidae)." *Records of the Australian Museum* 69, no. 3 (2017): 119-222. https://doi.org/10.3853j.2201-4349.69.2017.1666.

Calabrò, Concetta, Antonino Rindone, Clara Bertuccio, and Salvatore Giacobbe. "Hermaphroditism in a violet snail, *Janthina pallida* (Gastropoda, Caenogastropoda): a contribution." *Biologia* 5 (2019): 509-513. https://doi.org/10.2478/s11756-018-00177-9.

Heller, Joseph. *Sea Snails: A Natural History*. London: Springer, 2015.

Helm, Rebecca. "The mysterious ecosystem at the ocean's surface." *PLoS Biology* 19, no. 4 (2021): e3001046. https://doi.org/10.1371/journal.pbio.30-01046.

Lalli, Carol and Ronald Gilmer. *Pelagic Snails.* Redwood City: Stanford University Press, 1989.

Lesueur, Charles Alexandre and Nicolas-Martin Petit. *Voyage de découvertes aux Terres Australes exécuté par ordre de sa majesté l'Empereur et Roi, partie historique rédigée par M. F. Péron: Atlas par MM. Lesueur et Petit.* Paris: Imprimerie Impériale, 1807.

Sagiv, Gadi. "Deep Blue: Notes on the Jewish Snail Fight." *Contemporary Jewry* 35, no. 3 (October 2015): 285-313. https://www.jstor.org/stable/26345976.

Ward, Peter, Lewis Greenwald, and Olive Greenwald. "The Buoyancy of the Chambered Nautilus." *Scientific American* 243, no. 4 (October 1980): 190-203. https://www.jstor.org/stable/10.2307/24966441.

Wilson, D. P. and M. A. Wilson. "A contribution to the biology of *Ianthina* [sic] *janthina* (Linneus)." *Journal of the Marine Biological Association of the United Kingdom* 35 (1956): 291–305. https://doi.org/10.1017/S0025315400010146.

Acknowledgments

"How to Write a Protest Poem Amid a Pandemic" by Artress Bethany White originally appeared in *An Ecotone Almanac*, 2020, *Ecotone*.

About New Rivers Press

New Rivers Press emerged from a drafty Massachusetts barn in winter 1968. Intent on publishing work by new and emerging poets, founder C.W. "Bill" Truesdale labored for weeks over an old Chandler & Price letterpress to publish three hundred fifty copies of Margaret Randall's collection *So Many Rooms Has a House but One Roof*. About four hundred titles later, New Rivers is now a nonprofit learning press, based since 2001 at Minnesota State University Moorhead. Charles Baxter, one of the first authors with New Rivers, calls the press "the hidden backbone of the American literary tradition."

As a learning press, New Rivers guides student editors, designers, writers, and filmmakers through the various processes involved in selecting, editing, designing, publishing, and distributing literary books. In working, learning, and interning with New Rivers Press, students gain integral real-world knowledge that they bring with them into the publishing workforce at positions with publishers across the country, or to begin their own small presses and literary magazines.

Please visit our website: newriverspress.com for more information.